SpringerBriefs in Economics

For further volumes:
http://www.springer.com/series/8876

Carol Yeh-Yun Lin • Leif Edvinsson
Jeffrey Chen • Tord Beding

National Intellectual Capital and the Financial Crisis in Denmark, Finland, Iceland, Norway, and Sweden

Springer

Carol Yeh-Yun Lin
Department of Business Administration
National Chengchi University
Taipei, Taiwan

Leif Edvinsson
Universal Networking Intellectual Capital
Norrtälje, Sweden

Jeffrey Chen
Accenture
Chicago, IL
USA

Tord Beding
TC-Growth AB
Karlstad, Sweden

ISSN 2191-5504 ISSN 2191-5512 (electronic)
ISBN 978-1-4614-9535-2 ISBN 978-1-4614-9536-9 (eBook)
DOI 10.1007/978-1-4614-9536-9
Springer New York Heidelberg Dordrecht London

Library of Congress Control Number: 2013953292

Printed on acid-free paper

Springer is part of Springer Science+Business Media (www.springer.com)

Foreword I

The economic crisis is a consequence of many parallel factors which are all related to globalization and digitalization. My main concern, assessing this in more detail from the European perspective, is that revolutionary global forces have not been taken early nor seriously enough by most national and regional decision makers. The heads of European states and governments have once again recalled the importance of fiscal consolidation, structural reform, and targeted investment to put Europe back on the path of smart, sustainable, and inclusive growth. The main question is how capable and ready are the national governments to tackling the complex and manifold issues of crises and to renewing even radically many of our public and private structures and processes.

The first basic requirement is that all the European Union Member States remain fully committed to taking the actions required at the national level to achieve the objectives of the Europe 2020 Strategy. The second basic requirement is that the national and regional governments, as well as people, are ready for radical changes. This booklet, and the other 11 booklets by experienced authors, focus on national intellectual capital (NIC) and give necessary insights and facts for us, the readers, and especially for our in-depth systemic thinking of the interrelationships of NIC and economic recovery.

How should the national and regional decision makers tackle the existing knowledge of intangible capital? The focus needs to be more on the bottom-up approach stressing the developments on local and regional levels. I highlight our recent statements by the EU Committee of the Regions. The key priorities are to get more innovations out of research and to encourage mindset change toward open innovation.

The political decision makers are finally aware that the traditional indicators created for and used in industrial production cannot be applied to a knowledge-intensive, turbulent, and innovativeness-based global enterprise environment. Indicators that perceive the intangible dimensions of competitiveness – knowledge capital, innovation knowledge, and anticipation of the future – have been developed around the world, but their use has not yet become established in practice. This booklet accelerates the development and the use of these indicators.

This helps the local and regional, as well as central, governments in taking brave leaps forward on a practical level – giving greater ownership and involving all the stakeholders. This means the need of actions toward increasing the structural and relational capital of regions, both internally in communities of practice and in collaboration with others.

The new generation innovation activities are socially motivated, open and collectively participated, complex, and global by nature. The regions need to move toward open innovation, within a human-centered vision of partnerships between public and private sector actors, with universities playing a crucial role.

Regions should be encouraged to develop regional innovation platforms, which act as demand-based service centers and promote the use of international knowledge to implement the Europe 2020 Strategy, smart specialization, and European partnerships according to the interests and needs of regions. For this to happen, we need to apply the new dynamic understanding of regional innovation ecosystems, in which companies, cities, and universities as well as other public and private sector actors (the "Triple Helix") learn to work together in new and creative ways to fully harness their innovative potential.

New innovative practices do not come about by themselves. One major potential is the use of public procurement. The renewing of the European wide rules must increase the strategic agility and activities of municipalities and other public operators as creators of new solutions. Especially the execution of pre-commercial procurement should be reinforced even more in combination with open innovation to speed up the green knowledge society development, that is, for common reusable solutions in creating the infrastructures and services modern real-world innovation ecosystems are built upon. Conditions must be created that also allow for extensive development projects which address complex societal challenges and which take the form of risk-taking consortia.

One of our working instruments within the Committee of the Regions is the Europe 2020 Monitoring Platform, which broadly reviews and reflects the opinions and decisions on the regional level all around Europe. It gives a flavor of cultural and other socioeconomic differences inside the EU. This brings an important perspective to the intellectual capital, namely, the values and attitudes needed for citizens supporting policy makers on appropriate long-term investments and policies.

Emphasizing the importance of these issues, decision makers in all countries and regions need a deep and broad understanding of the critical success factors affecting the national intellectual capital. With all the facts and frames for thinking, this booklet gives a valuable insight into today's challenges.

Markku Markkula
Advisor to the Aalto University Presidents
Member of the EU Committee of the Regions
Former Member of the Parliament of Finland

Foreword II

Financial crisis – words very much heard today. What is all this about, actually, and how to get a grip on what we experience today? This booklet gives an important insight on the factors affecting competitiveness and productivity in modern knowledge society. We need to see behind the obvious, and we need to have increasingly "qualified guesses" as the character of the society and industry has fundamentally changed.

What is very important to notice is the shift toward intangible value creation beyond the deterministic phenomena we saw very clearly in the industrial era. Cost drivers were the important ones throughout the industry. Mass production, bigger is better, very traditional productivity factors was the mantra.

However, the production picture is changing. Increasingly value is created by the intangibles, often services related to the tangible components, and even totally in immaterial value creation, where perceptions and expectations determine the market value of the "extended product." We also see rapid change in organizational forms, we see new types of entrepreneurship growing besides the traditional industry clusters, we see smart specialization of regions and countries.

This means also that there will be clearly different and complementary roles of the actors in innovation and value creation ecosystems. Large companies, small ones, and even microenterprises together with the public sector are traditionally seen as the active partners in such innovation environments. The real issue in the dynamic markets is however that the end users are increasingly to be taken on board as *active subjects* for innovation and not merely treated as objects, customers. Markets need to be shaped and created in a much more dynamic way than ever before. Open innovation beyond cross-licensing includes the societal capital as an important intangible engine for productivity growth. Innovation happens only when the offering is meeting the demand. Otherwise, we can only speak about inventions or ideas.

We need to have a close look at the intellectual capital and the different factors within it when we design our policy approaches. Short-term investments in process capital (infrastructures) and market capital seem to be very important for the manufacturing base as such, but at the same time measures for longer-term intellectual capital development and efficiency need to be taken.

Increasingly important is the *structure* and the open *processes* related to intangible capital and knowledge pools. For sustainable long-term development, both the *human capital and renewal capital are crucial*, as they are directly related to the innovation capability of the region. The correlation between these factors and the GDP growth is indisputable. In knowledge-intensive industries, talent is attracting talent, and the connectivity which modern ICT provides makes this talent pool fluid across disciplines, organizations, and geographical settings. It is imperative to modernize the innovation systems enabling the full dynamics needed for success in knowledge-intensive industries, beyond the traditional boundaries.

Measuring the performance of innovation systems becomes increasingly complex due to the mash-up of different disciplines, having new types of actors and interactions between them. Hence, the importance of analysis of the various components of the national intellectual capital (and equally on national innovation capability) as done in this booklet cannot be underestimated when making qualified guesses for operational choices to create functioning innovation ecosystems. The only predictable in true innovation is the unpredictability and the surprises. The role of the public sector is to drive strategy and measures enabling the unpredictable, and to catalyse a fluid, seamless and frictionless innovation system to grow, with strong interplay with the surrounding society.

We need to have courage to experiment, to prototype in real-world settings, to have all stakeholders involved to find and remove the friction points of innovation, and to achieve sustainable innovation ecosystems for knowledge-intensive products and services.

I wish you interesting reading with this mind-opening report.

Bror Salmelin
Advisor, Innovation Systems
European Commission
DG CONNECT

Foreword III

The 2008 global financial crisis hit the whole world with unprecedented speed, causing widespread financial panic. Consumer confidence dropped to the lowest level since the Great Depression. Taiwan, with an export-dependent economy, was seriously impacted by the crisis and the unemployment rate hiked while household consumption levels dropped. At the onset of the financial crisis, Professor Lin was the Dean of Student Affairs at National Chengchi University in Taipei, Taiwan. She was in charge of financial aid and student loans and thus saw firsthand the direct impact the financial crisis had upon the students. The crisis was so devastating that Professor Lin, along with the university, was compelled to launch several new initiatives to raise money and help students weather the difficult times.

I am very glad that she took this painful experience to heart and set herself upon the task of investigating the impact of the crisis, trying to look into the causes and consequences for policy implications, not only for Taiwan but for an array of 48 countries. In particular, she approaches the crisis from the perspective of "national intellectual capital," which is very important in today's knowledge-driven economy.

Taiwan is an example of a knowledge economy and has enjoyed the fame of being referred to as a "high-tech island." Without an abundance of natural resources, Taiwan's hardworking and highly educated population is the single most precious resource that the island has. Acknowledging the value of such human resources and intellectual capital, the Taiwan Intellectual Capital Research Center (TICRC) was established under my leadership in 2003. Since then, Taiwan's government has continuously funded the university to conduct relevant research projects aimed at enhancing the intellectual capital of Taiwan. Having been thus endowed with the responsibility of nourishing future leaders in the public and private sectors, we have focused on building up our strength in innovation, entrepreneurship, and technology management-related research and education.

To enhance intellectual capital research, we recently formed a joint team of professors for a 4-year project in order to leverage their respective research capabilities. Through this project, we hope to provide policy suggestions for the government by exploring the creativity, innovation, and intellectual capital at national, regional, city, and county levels. The goal is to come up with an intangible assets agenda for Taiwan's future sustainability. Professor Lin is an integral member in this research team.

Following her 2011 book, *National Intellectual Capital: A Comparison of 40 Countries*, this booklet series is Professor Lin's second attempt at presenting her research, conducted under the sponsorship of TICRC, to international readers. As the Founding Director of TICRC and her President, I am honored to give a brief introduction of the value of this booklet series.

In comparison to her 2011 book, this series increased the number of countries studied to 48 and particularly focuses on the impact of intellectual capital on the 2008 global financial crisis. Rarely has an economic issue been systematically studied from the viewpoint of intangible assets, particularly at such a large scale of 48 countries. The research results show without a doubt that national intellectual capital is indeed an important economic development enhancer. In particular, the fact that countries with higher national intellectual capital experienced faster recoveries from the 2008 financial crisis provides a strong message for the policy makers.

In addition to providing insights into national policy, the booklet also summarizes the background of each country before the crisis, the key events during the crisis, economic development afterward, and future prospects and challenges. Each volume affords readers a holistic picture of what happened in each country in an efficient manner. The linkage between national intellectual capital and this financial crisis also provides a different perspective of the crisis.

I am happy that Professor Lin continues to share her valuable research results with international readers. I sincerely hope that her insights garner more attention concerning the benefits of developing national intellectual capital for the well-being of every nation.

Se-Hwa Wu
Professor, Graduate Institute of Technology
and Innovation Management
President, National Chengchi University,
Taipei, Taiwan

Preface I

There are "mounting risks of a breakup of the Euro zone." Such comments are frequent today on how the European leaders are handling the escalating crisis and its potential impact on non-European countries. But few leaders, reporters, or researchers are actually addressing the situation of national intellectual capital (NIC) and its signals. In addition to the financial crisis, is there an emerging NIC crisis as well? Why is it emerging? How should policy makers think about NIC? In what way does it need specific attention? When will the outcome and impact of taken NIC policy steps be realized?

In the midst of the European crisis, there are national interventions to address the issues mentioned above. In leading economic nations, the investments going into intangibles now exceed tangibles and are positively correlated to income per capita. However, these still do not show up clearly in national mapping as well as policy-making insights. Therefore, the New Club of Paris is focusing the knowledge agenda setting for countries on societal innovation (see www.new-club-of-paris.org).

Chairman Ben Bernanke of the US Federal Reserve addressed some of these same aspects in a keynote speech in May 2011 hosted by Georgetown University: http://www.icapitaladvisors.com/2011/05/31/bernanke-on-intangible-capital/. OECD and the World Bank are developing NIC statistics, often based on the model from Corrado-Hultén. Japan has been developing both NIC and intangible assets (IA) at METI for some time now. Their research on IC/IA has resulted in a National IA Week with various key stakeholders, such as government agencies, universities, stock exchange, and enterprises. Japan is so far the only country in the world to hold such activities, and they have been doing so for the last 8 years. Australia, Singapore, South Korea, and China are currently undertaking various NIC initiatives. Other countries are also becoming more and more aware of NIC, with policy rhetoric centered on innovation, education, R&D, and trade. Despite this, the map for a more justified NIC navigation has been missing.

This booklet highlights NIC development for a number of countries, based on 48 different indicators, aggregated into four major NIC components of human capital, market capital, process capital, and renewal capital. The model here is a refined and verified statistical model in comparison to the Corrado-Hultén model.

We call it the L-E-S model after the contributors Lin–Edvinsson–Stahle. Based on a deeper understanding and the timeline pattern it sets forth, this model will add to a better NIC navigation, not to mention knowledge agenda setting for countries.

Upon looking at a global cluster NIC map, it is evident that the top leading countries seem to be small countries, especially Singapore, the Nordic countries, Hong Kong, and Taiwan. For the USA, Finland, and Sweden, around 50 % or more of their economic growth is related to NIC aspects. Sweden, Finland, Switzerland, the USA, Israel, and Denmark are strongly influenced in their GDP growth by focusing on renewal capital.

It might be that we will see a clearer map of the NIC ecosystem and drivers for wealth emerge in the extension of this ongoing unique research of NIC. This booklet will present an NIC map for various clusters of countries. It can be used for benchmarking as well as bench learning for policy prototyping. The starting point is awareness and thinking of NIC and its drivers for economic results. Based on this more refined navigation, NIC metrics can be presented.

A deeper understanding will emerge from this research, such as the scaling up of limited skilled human capital in one nation by using the globalized broadband technologies for migration and flow of knowledge (such as telemedicine or mobile banking in Africa). This is also referred to as the IC multiplier. It might also be the way the old British Commonwealth was constructed, but without the IC taxonomy. In modern taxonomy, it might be the shaping of NIC alliances for the migration and flow of IC between nations.

Another understanding that might emerge for policy making is the issue of employment versus unemployment. The critical understanding will be the deployment of IC drivers. This will require another networked workforce of value networkers on a global scale, such as volunteering software and apps developers. However, such volunteers do not show up in traditional statistics for the mapping on behalf of policy makers.

On another level, there might be a clear gap analysis between nations to support the vision process of a nation. On a deeper level, it is also a leadership responsibility to address the gap of NIC positions versus potential positions. Such a gap is in fact a liability to the citizens, to be addressed in due time.

This will take us to the need for the continuous renewal of social systems. The so-called Arab Spring is explained by some as resulting from three drivers: lack of renewal of social systems, the Internet, and soccer as cross-class interaction space. The lack of social renewal and innovation is most likely critical early warning signals. For Greece, we can see such a tipping point occurred back in 1999.

On a global scale, we might see that the concern for the Euro zone crisis can and should be explained by a deeper and supplementary understanding of national intellectual capital, in addition to financial capital. So we need to refine our understanding of NIC mapping, NIC metrics, and NIC organizational constructs into societal innovation for the benefit of wealth creation of subsequent generations.

Leif Edvinsson
The World's First Professor of Intellectual Capital
Chairman and Cofounder of New Club of Paris

Preface II

Our first book *National Intellectual Capital: A Comparison of 40 Countries* was published in early 2011, at a time when the 2008 global financial crisis had been declared over; yet, the European region was still plagued with sovereign debt problems. Before we finalized the book, we were able to retrieve some of our raw data concerning the troubled countries, such as Greece, Iceland, Ireland, Portugal, and Spain. The results of our analysis based on data spanning 1995 to 2008 revealed some early warning signs of the financial turmoil in those countries. In my preface of that book, I mentioned the warning signs might reveal only the tip of an iceberg. At that time, my coauthor Professor Edvinsson and I decided to do a follow-up study to trace the development of national intellectual capital (NIC) in as many countries as possible, particularly through the lens of the 2008 global financial crisis. This 12 booklet series is the result of that determination.

The 2008 global financial crisis came with unexpected speed and had a widespread effect that surprised many countries far from the epicenter of the initial US subprime financial problem, geographically and financially. According to reports, no country was immune to the impact of this financial crisis. Such development clearly signifies how closely connected the world has become and the importance of having a global interdependent view. By reporting what happened during 2005–2010 in 48 major countries throughout the world, this booklet series serves the purpose of uncovering national problems before the crisis, government coping strategies, stimulus plans, potential prospects and challenges of each individual country, and the interdependence between countries. The data for 6 years allows us to compare NIC and economic development crossing before, during, and after the financial crisis. These are handy booklets for readers to have a quick yet overall view of countries of personal interest. The list of 48 countries in 11 clusters is provided in the appendix of each booklet.

Searching for financial crisis-related literature for 48 countries is itself a very daunting task, not to mention summarizing and analyzing it. For financial crisis-related literature, we mainly relied on the reports and statistics of certain world organizations, including OECD, World Bank, United Nations, International Monetary Fund (IMF), European Commission Office, the US Congressional Research

Service, the US Central Intelligence Agency, and International Labor Office (ILO). Some reliable research centers, such as the National Bureau of Economic Research in the USA, World Economic Forum, the Heritage Foundation in the USA, and government websites from each country, were also our sources of information. Due to the requirement of more up-to-date and comprehensive information, we were not able to use as much academic literature as we would have liked, because it generally covers a very specific topic with time lag and with research methods not easily comprehended by the general public. Therefore, we had to resort to some online news reports for more current information.

In the middle of 2012, the lasting financial troubles caused the European economy to tilt back into a recession, which also slowed down economic growth across the globe. However, almost 4 years have passed since the outbreak of the global financial crisis in late 2008; it is about time to reflect on what happened and the impact of the financial crisis. By comparing so many countries, we came to a preliminary conclusion that countries with faster recovery from the financial crisis have higher national intellectual capital than those with slower recovery. In other words, countries that rebounded fast from the crisis generally have solid NIC fundamentals, including human capital, market capital, process capital, and renewal capital. We also found that the higher the NIC, the higher the GDP per capita (ppp). This booklet series provides a different perspective to look beyond the traditional economic indicators for national development.

In an era when intangible assets have become a key competitive advantage, investing in national intellectual capital development is investing in future national development and well-being.

Enjoy!

Carol Yeh-Yun Lin
Professor, Department of Business Administration
National Chengchi University, Taiwan
Taiwan Intellectual Capital Research Center (TICRC)

Executive Summary

Proper positioning in the international markets is a crucial strategic issue, especially for small economies.

How can national intellectual capital (NIC) act as a policy guideline for national well-being? One of the key causes of the 2008 financial crisis was the failure of conventional financial metrics and accounting systems to detect potential risks due to nontransparent information disclosure. To address the importance of intangibles, the US Bureau of Economic Analysis has initiated a new metrics approach to be more focused on intangibles, effective from July 1, 2013. For example, R&D will be regarded as investment rather than expense.

Our earlier national intellectual capital (NIC) research revealed warning signs of the financial crisis for Greece, Iceland, and Ireland. Such findings indicate that NIC, albeit intangible, can provide valuable insights into risk control and strategy formulation. This booklet looks at the connections between the financial crisis and NIC development for Denmark, Finland, Iceland, Norway, and Sweden.

In particular, this report attempts to answer the following questions: How did these countries weather the 2008 global financial crisis? What happened to Iceland and caused its financial meltdown? Why were the Nordic countries, like Denmark, Finland, and Sweden, more resilient to this financial shock than other advanced countries? What are the NIC profiles of these countries? What role has NIC played in the national development of these countries? What is the long-term sustainability of their present good NIC position? Are there any early warning signs to observe for NIC navigation in the future?

Data covering 2005–2010 for 48 countries indicates that **the higher the NIC, the higher the GDP per capita (ppp)**, accentuating the value of NIC as a driver in major countries throughout the world. **For the 6-year average of NIC rankings among 48 countries, Denmark ranks third, Finland fourth, Iceland eighth, Norway ninth, and Sweden first.** Despite the financial crisis, these countries are for the moment in the top ten positions in terms of NIC out of the 48 countries.

The 2008 financial crisis caused severe impacts across the globe and is considered to be the worst financial crisis since the Great Depression of the 1930s.

The crisis came with unexpected speed, resulting in global economic shock and consequently a number of bank failures. During this period, economies worldwide slowed, credits tightened, and international trade declined. In an effort to mitigate the crisis, governments and central banks across the globe responded with unprecedented fiscal stimuli, monetary policy expansions, and institutional bailouts. These measures had their desired impact, and the financial crisis was declared over by the end of 2009.

However, the short global recovery in 2010 was overshadowed by the lingering sovereign debt problems in Europe; thus, a global economic slowdown recurred in the second half of 2011. Despite the efforts of European leaders to prevent large economies like Italy and Spain from needing bailouts, Spain still requested external financial assistance in June 2012. Although the global economic outlook for 2013 will be better than that of 2012, growth in the Nordic countries (except Sweden) was still predicted to be weak in 2013. Hopefully, the global economy will pick up in 2014 if the expected global economy upturn is realized.

In retrospect, Iceland's financial meltdown was mainly due to the overexpansion of its banks in foreign markets and the heavy borrowing of consumers and businesses in foreign currencies. For such a small economy, its foreign exposure became unsustainable with loans and other assets totaling more than ten times the country's GDP. The problem was so serious that when the international money market dried up, its government had no ability to bail them out.

The other four Nordic countries weathered this financial crisis relatively well due to the following reasons. Denmark entered the recession with a strong fiscal position and a sound fiscal policy framework. Its large budget surpluses and a positive net asset position helped the country cope with the crisis. In addition, Danish mortgage bonds were a liability to the mortgage bank issuing them and were supported by the capital, reserves, and income of the banks as well as by their collateral. With the system, the bond holders were well protected by the entire resources of the banks.

Finland's financial system is highly internationalized, making it very vulnerable to the deterioration in global financial markets. Nonresidents own about 80 % of the publicly traded companies, and about one-quarter of the businesses is invested by nonresidents. As a result, Finland was among the hardest hit by this crisis. Fortunately, the solvency of all Finnish banks exceeded the statutory requirement of 8 %; the regulation and management of its banking sector was much more sophisticated than during the previous financial crisis in the early 1990s. These preconditions helped the country recover from the crisis relatively fast. In addition, Finland's NIC was high; especially its innovation-related renewal capital (RC) ranked number three, next to Switzerland and Sweden. The country is also known for its commitment for continuous cultivation of innovation ecosystems, which has helped build a more resilient economy.

Being the richest country among the 48 we studied, the Norwegian government adopted the most ambitious fiscal policy measures in more than 30 years at the onset of the global financial crisis. Stimulus package from petroleum revenues was estimated to be around US$20.8 billion (NOK 130 billion), providing large financial room for maneuvering. Extensive measures to stabilize the financial markets were established and worked very well.

Sweden's prudent fiscal management in the years prior to the global economic turmoil created fiscal space for some stimulus measures, including labor market support and social security tax cuts. During the crisis, its fast interest rate cuts, swift policy measures, public sector transformation, as well as exceptional government support to the financial system helped contain the length and depth of the recession. Although Sweden ranked number two in renewal capital in this study, its decline since 2008 is a warning signal for future sustainability, especially in this increasingly knowledge- and innovation-dominated global economy.

In general, sound macroeconomic systems reformed after their 1990s Nordic crisis, and the swift policy responses by their governments had helped these countries recover from this global financial crisis faster than first expected.

Most of the Global Competitiveness Index (GCI, Figure 1.1) ranking of the Nordic countries declined, except Sweden. When the rankings of 2005–2006 and 2011–2012 were compared, Denmark dropped from 4 to 8, Finland from 1 to 4, Iceland from 7 to 30, and Norway from 9 to 16, but Sweden remained at 3. The **real GDP growth** pattern of these countries was largely similar – dropping to negative growth in both 2008 (except Finland) and 2009 and then rebounding to positive growth in 2010. Specifically, Norway experienced less GDP growth fluctuation over the 6 years. Finland and Iceland had the deepest drop in 2009, yet Iceland rebounded slower in 2010 due to its financial turmoil. Unexpectedly, the richest country in this study - Norway still had a negative GDP growth in 2010.

In terms of general **government debt**, Iceland more than doubled its precrisis debt level in 2010. The other four Nordic countries had very steady debt levels during and after the financial crisis. Aside from GDP growth and government debt, **unemployment** and its social impact are among the major concerns of the financial crisis. From 2009, the unemployment rate of the Nordic countries (except Norway) rose, with Denmark and Iceland having the greatest jump, followed by Finland and Sweden. Unexpectedly, Norway even reduced its unemployment rate during and after the financial crisis compared with its precrisis level. **Consumer price inflation** (CPI) of these Nordic countries (except Iceland) had some increases in 2008, dropped in 2009, and then resumed to precrisis levels in 2010. Iceland had much higher CPI than the other four countries through this period. Its 6.69 % CPI in 2006 was already a warning signal. After the financial crisis, its CPI has reduced to 5.4 % in 2010 from its peak of 12.65 % in 2008.

For NIC component capitals, over the studied 6 years (2005–2010), **human capital** (HC) did not vary much among these countries. However, Finland consistently had the lowest HC over the years, even though its student PISA performance was the highest in this group. The **market capital** (MC) of these countries was relatively stable over the years, except for Iceland. The **process capital** (PC) was also relatively stable, except again for Iceland. The **renewal capital** (RC) formed three groups. Consistently, Finland and Sweden were in the top group, Denmark and Iceland in the middle group, and Norway by itself had the lowest renewal capital during this period. The **financial capital** (based on a 1–10 scale) did not show much difference among these five countries. However, consistently Norway had the highest score. For the overall **NIC**, in 2010, Denmark, Finland, and Sweden were in the high group; Norway by itself in the middle; and Iceland dropped to the lowest due to its financial turmoil.

The co-development pattern of NIC-GDP, MC-GDP, and PC-GDP was largely the same – Denmark, Finland, and Sweden had intertwined development paths; Iceland had a backward horizontal path; and Norway was apart from the rest of the countries with a tilt toward the GDP axis. For HC-GDP co-development, Finland was by itself in the lower part of the graph. For RC-GDP co-development, Finland and Sweden were at the higher end of the RC axis, followed by Denmark, Iceland, and Norway. As for long-term NIC (HC + RC), Sweden had both high HC and high RC, Denmark and Iceland had high HC and middle RC, Finland had middle HC and high RC, and Norway had middle HC and low RC. For short-term NIC (MC + PC), the Nordic countries were clustered together at the high, high end of the graph, except Iceland which had a watershed decline in both MC and PC.

For **dynamic NIC ranking** changes in three time periods (2005–2006, 2007–2008, 2009–2010), the ranking gains represent increasing international competitiveness (among the 48 countries) after the financial crisis. Sweden gained the greatest international competitiveness in market capital after the financial crisis, followed by Norway. Finland gained the greatest international competitiveness in process capital after the financial crisis, followed by Sweden. Iceland had the greatest ranking loss in market capital, followed by process capital and overall NIC. Unexpectedly, Denmark lost international competitiveness after the financial crisis in market capital and process capital on a relatively large scale.

NIC 3D **trajectory analysis** was conducted to detect the enhancing and impeding factors of each country in reaching a targeted GDP per capita (ppp), benchmarking Switzerland due to its high NIC and financial performance among the 48 countries. To reach the GDP level of Switzerland, Iceland has the longest distance (−67.78 %) to cover, followed by Norway (−43.84 %), Denmark (−28.28 %), Sweden (−20.47 %), and Finland (−20.20 %). Interestingly, even though Denmark consistently had a better performance than Finland intangibly (NIC) and tangibly (GDP), its distance to the targeted Switzerland was farther than Finland. A likely answer is the difference in renewal capital. Although Denmark was ranked number one in both human capital and process capital, its renewal capital was ranked sixth. Nevertheless, Denmark's science policy transformation adopted 10 years ago for heavier R&D investment was found to have gradual effect in recent years. Finland's human capital, market capital, process capital, and financial capital all ranked lower than Denmark's; however, its renewal capital ranked number three among 48 countries, closer to Switzerland's number one. This finding clearly indicates how important "renewal capital" is to advanced countries.

As of mid-2013, the economic activities of the Nordic countries were impacted by the prolonged financial uncertainty in the Euro area. Although these countries (except Iceland) showed their resilience during this financial crisis, challenges still lie ahead as described in Chap. 5.

The 2008 global financial crisis provided an ideal opportunity for nations to examine/renew/innovate the soundness of their economic system and the effectiveness of **national governance related to NIC and Societal Wealth development**. The following implications are drawn from our research findings. Readers can refer to Chap. 5 for the rationale behind these implications.

1. Maintaining a sound financial system is an endless job to navigate and withstand future financial shock.
2. Proper positioning in the international markets is a crucial strategic issue, especially for small economies.
3. Government's timely and strong leadership is critical for restoring public confidence when financial crisis unfolds.
4. Adopting smart and value-creating investments in economic downturn will further enhance national well-being.
5. Straightening the aftermath exit transition is essential to continuously benefit from the extra resources allocated through stimulus package during the financial crisis.
6. Establishing a network of regional alliance for mutual support may reduce future risks.
7. Dynamically balancing various pulling forces may create a better environment and NIC ecosystem for future national development.
8. Relying on a single source for national development is too risky for future sustainability.
9. Enhancing the added value of national intellectual capital may help sustain the Nordic countries.
10. Attending to NIC development pattern over time through societal intelligence helps point out a better navigation direction for coping measures.

This report reveals that Denmark needs to pay more attention to its losing international competitiveness in market capital and process capital after the financial crisis. In addition, its continuous decline in Global Competitiveness Index (GCI), from 4 in 2005–2006 to 8 in 2011–2012 further to 12 in 2012–2013, also sent a signal for coping measures. Finland advanced its process capital after the financial crisis, which built a better infrastructure and ecosystem for the knowledge economy. However, with its relatively low financial capital, enhancing the added value of its high intangible assets must be considered. Iceland dropped heavily in both its intangible and tangible assets due to its financial turmoil. Although recovery is under way, its competitiveness has not yet recovered, as the newly released 2012–2013 GCI still rated Iceland 30, the same as its 2011–2012 ranking. Norway can work on upgrading its NIC to a higher level, as the country consistently lagged behind its peers in intangible assets that future competitiveness relies on. Sweden recovered the best from this financial crisis among the Nordic countries. Up until 2010, its long-term NIC was still higher than that of other Nordic countries and its short-term NIC had great advancement after this global financial crisis. These findings indicate that Sweden achieved a more balanced development in all four capitals (HC, MC, PC, and RC). However, the newly released 2012–2013 GCI ranked Sweden fourth, one rank lower than in 2011–2012. Sweden's declining renewal capital was revealed in this study, and the call for R&D and universities research reform by Swedish scholars has sent an early warning that deserves some attention.

In general, the Nordic countries have encountered institutional reform, high unemployment (especially youth unemployment), as well as age-related challenges. Solutions to these problems may lie in measures through societal innovation, apprentice system, flexicurity labor policy, and collaboration between the public and private sectors.

In an era when the intangible asset has become a key competitive advantage, investing in national intellectual capital development is, in essence, investing in future national development and well-being. National intellectual capital should be nourished from both a local cultural viewpoint and that of global interconnectivity by social media. Based on emerging new insights of values, societal history, and citizen relationships, a key focus for the future will be on the fusion of national intellectual capital and social service innovation as well as societal innovation, for the enabling of a new societal fabric.

Contents

List of Figures

List of Tables

Chapter 1
Introduction

In April 2013, the International Monetary Fund (2013) reported that global prospects have improved, but the road of recovery in the advanced economies will remain bumpy. World output growth was predicted to reach 3.25 % in 2013 and 4 % in 2014. In the major advanced economies, activity is expected to gradually accelerate with the USA taking the lead. However, risks remain in the Euro area pertaining to adjustment fatigue, insufficient institutional reform, and prolonged stagnation (IMF, 2013). In the emerging Asia, exports in China were hurt by the weak market in Europe and its growth slowed. For Nordic countries, Nordea (2013) projected 1.2 % and 2.0 % economic growth for 2013 and 2014, respectively, up from 1.0 % growth in 2012.

The aftermath of the 2008 global financial crisis varies from country to country. Some have recovered from the turmoil and are picking up growth, such as the countries introduced in this volume. Some are still struggling to stand on their feet financially, such as Greece and Portugal. In hindsight, it is valuable to reflect what had happened during the last few years in different countries to gain some insights for future prevention.

What started off as subprime mortgage problems in the financial sector of the USA snowballed into the deepest and most widespread financial and economic crisis of the last eight decades. With almost synchronized worldwide recession, global GDP contracted for the first time since World War II. Governments and central banks around the world responded to the crisis through both conventional and unconventional fiscal and monetary measures in order to maintain financial order and help industries, private companies, and citizens wade through the difficulties.

In 2009, the World Bank predicted that the 2008 global financial crisis would create an additional 53 million poor who live under US$2 per day, due mainly to the decline of global economic growth. The magnitude of the crisis was so huge that it disrupted the global financial system, and consequently there was no single economy in the world that was completely isolated from the effect of the crisis.

In the wake of the crisis, causes of the disaster have become known, although its magnitude varied from country to country after combining with local factors.

C.Y.-Y. Lin et al., *National Intellectual Capital and the Financial Crisis in Denmark, Finland, Iceland, Norway, and Sweden*, SpringerBriefs in Economics,
DOI 10.1007/978-1-4614-9536-9_1,

Briefly speaking, the collapse of subprime bonds in the USA resulted in shortage in the global money market and huge amounts of foreign investments were withdrawn from invested countries all over the world to meet their headquarters' liquidity. Thus, the credit squeeze affected domestic market operations. Due to the very negative cash flow position, many companies slashed their production levels and cancelled or postponed investment projects (Mendonça, 2010). With the tight monetary market, export demands dropped and unemployment increased. Adding to the scene was overlending and overspending by some European Union countries even before 2008. Consequently, banks in many countries did not have enough money to support the repayment of foreign debts and corporate loans. Then, confidence fell, which directly hit the consumer market, and a global financial crisis set in.

One key factor that did not prevent the financial crisis from happening was that the conventional financial system failed to detect the potential troubles of subprime bonds, very likely due to nontransparent information disclosure. Therefore, at the early stage of the crisis, management scholars criticized the inability of the traditional accounting system to reveal intangible assets that explain hidden values as well as risks for proper decision making (Reavis, 2009). In line with such criticism, intellectual capital (Edvinsson & Malone, 1997) advocates the values of intangible assets and has gained increasing attention in today's keener global competition. After the financial crisis, the Chief Adviser at Tekes, the Finnish Funding Agency for Technology and Innovation, pointed out, "In the future, intangible assets, such as patents, advertising, education and training, are highlighted increasingly as a source of growth" (Palkamo, 2011).

It is our deep belief that national intellectual capital, albeit intangible, can provide valuable insight to policy makers regarding future risk control and strategy formulation. Our book *National Intellectual Capital: A Comparison of 40 Countries* (Lin & Edvinsson, 2011; www.nic40.org) was born out of this belief and traced the national intellectual capital development of 40 countries over 14 years (1995–2008). The data analysis revealed certain warning signs of financial troubles for countries such as Greece, Iceland, and Ireland (Lin & Edvinsson, 2011, pp. 327–333). As a follow-up study, this booklet series is an attempt to further understand the relationships between the 2008 global financial crisis and national intellectual capital (NIC) development.

The booklet series, in its entirety, examine the national intellectual capital statuses of 48 countries from the period of 2005–2010 to glean new understanding about whether there is a NIC development pattern that distinguishes fast recovery countries from ones with slow recovery. This is presented through a series of 11 country clusters, with one booklet focusing on one particular cluster. The clusters are decided based upon several factors: geographical proximity, similar size, or similar phase of economic development. Focusing on one cluster at a time, we first probe within a single country and then extend to comparisons between multiple countries to see whether the situation before and after the crisis can be explained by intangible NIC. Our data comes from the well-recognized International Institute for Management Development (IMD) in Switzerland. The IMD has been publishing yearly rankings of World Competitiveness for around two decades. Hopefully, the analysis in this booklet series can provide a different perspective of the financial crisis for future policy implications.

This volume, Volume 11, focuses on the five Nordic countries of Denmark, Finland, Iceland, Norway, and Sweden. In what follows, this booklet provides the economic background of these five countries as a whole before going into each individual country's development. Through this process, the authors hope to paint a general picture of the economic condition and provide a basis for our dataset and analysis in future sections.

Chapter 2 briefly introduces the impact of the 2008 financial crisis on the five countries. Chapter 3 discusses the NIC development of these five countries. Chapter 4 describes issues beyond the financial crisis and Chap. 5 concludes with future perspective and policy implications.

Economic Background

Since the economic history of these five countries goes back centuries, it is impossible to cover the entire spectrum in our work. As such, this background discussion will consider events in the relative recent history from 2005 onward that have the most direct impact upon the current economic conditions of each specific country. In addition, particular attention will be given to the 2008 financial crisis. In doing so, the authors hope that the background, in conjunction with our later data and analysis, will provide a "before, during, and after" picture of what was happening from a macroeconomic and intangible assets viewpoint.

For these countries particularly, the early 1990s Nordic banking crisis needs to be briefly reviewed as it exerts a lot of influence on the financial practices of the Nordic region afterward. According to Ingves (2002), this Nordic banking problem was the first systemic crisis in industrialized countries since the 1930s. In the 1980s, the financial systems of Finland, Norway, and Sweden underwent major deregulation. The financial liberalization set off a lending boom, capital inflows, rising asset prices, rapidly increasing consumption and investment, and an overheated non-tradable sectors (Jonung, 2010). Around 1990, the boom turned into a bust with capital outflows, widespread bankruptcies, falling employment, declining investments, negative GDP growth, systemic banking crises, currency crises, and depression (Jonung, 2010).

In the wake of this banking crisis, the monitoring of domestic financial stability was placed high on the policy agendas of all the Nordic countries (Ingves, 2002), and regularly assessing strengths and vulnerabilities of a country's financial sector has become a common practice. The Nordic experiences also revealed the importance of operational restructuring of corporations as the underpinning of bank restructuring. In coping with the financial crisis, the Nordic experience indicated the need for prominent state involvement in the resolution process: it was the state rather than the private sector that had to lead the systemic restructuring exercise seeking to bring in private-sector owners and investors as much as possible (Ingves, 2001). In the late 1990s, the IMF tested the crisis management system developed after this Nordic crisis and proved it worked well in the 1997–1998 Asian crisis with some adaptations for different countries.

The Nordic financial system was tested again in the 2008 global financial crisis. In 2012, while some European Union countries were still trapped in financial turmoil, the Nordic countries had already recovered from the crisis. Even Iceland had emerged from its banking meltdown. To paint a general picture of their global competitiveness in the most recent years and before the financial crisis, we introduce the Global Competitiveness Index (GCI) published by the World Economic Forum for the reader's reference. This index is relatively robust as it takes into account the 12 distinct pillars[1] containing basic requirements, efficiency enhancers, and innovation factors that contribute to a nation's overall economic strength. Based upon commonly accepted economic theory, the development of a total of 142 countries was split into three stages in which different factors play the dominant role in determining the outcome of a country's economy. Stage 1, Stage 2, and Stage 3 are respectively characterized by being factor, efficiency, and innovation driven (Schwab, 2011). These five countries were all categorized as Stage 3 economies.

Plotting each country's annual ranking against a time series of seven periods, Fig. 1.1 displays a rough pictorial overview of these five countries' global competitiveness before and after the financial crisis. As an indicator of economic strength comparing ranking between 2005–2006 and 2011–2012, Denmark dropped from 4 to 8, Finland from 1 to 4, Iceland from 7 to 30, Norway from 9 to 16, and Sweden remained the same at 3. Over the years, all the Nordic countries (except Sweden) declined in GCI ranking, especially with Norway and Iceland having a more drastic drop. The sharp slide of Iceland's GCI is clearly associated with its financial collapse. Yet, Norway's losing global competitiveness deserves some attention. Figure 1.1 uncovers a serious issue of whether the Nordic countries can sustain their competitiveness in the future with fiercer global competition.

In September 2011, the OECD reported that major economies were tilting back into recession as sovereign debt problems continued to ail the Euro zone (Bryant, 2011). Concerns about the fiscal and banking problems continued to weigh on the global economic outlook. Economic activity contracted further in Europe (Reserve Bank of Australia [RBA], 2012), and the US economy experienced only modest growth. However, much of the developing world had relatively strong growth.

In January 2012, World Bank (2012) suggested that developing countries prepare for further downside risks, as Euro Area debt problems and weak growth in several big emerging economies were dimming global growth prospects. The

[1] The 12 pillars include institutions, infrastructure, macroeconomic environment, health and primary education, higher education and training, goods market efficiency, labor market efficiency, financial market development, technological readiness, market size, business sophistication, and innovation.

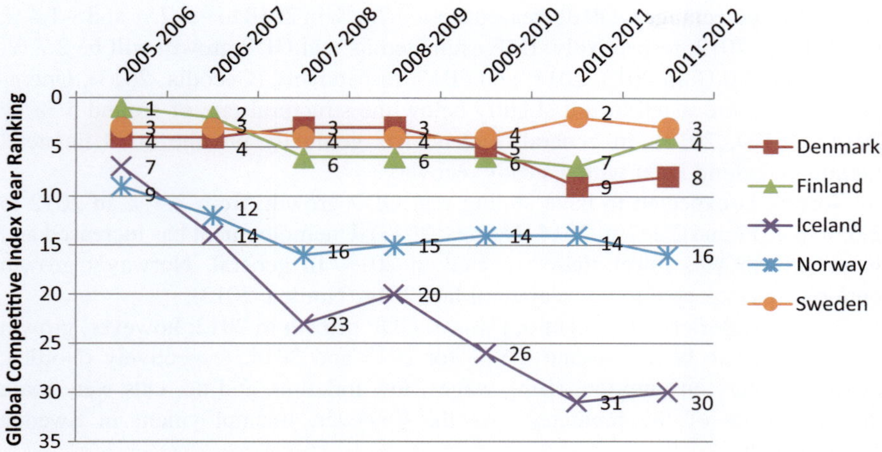

Fig. 1.1 GCI ranking of the five Nordic countries

World Bank also lowered its growth forecast for 2012 to 5.4 % for developing countries and 1.4 % for high-income countries (−0.3 % for the Euro Area), down from its previous estimates of 6.2 % and 2.7 % (1.9 % for the Euro Area), respectively. It also predicted that "an escalation of the crisis would spare no-one. Developed- and developing-country growth rates could fall by as much or more than in 2008/09."

The economies in Nordic countries slowed in 2012, except Norway. In 2013, Nordic countries were picking up growth, except for Finland and Norway. Denmark, with −0.5 % real GDP growth in 2012, was reported to be expecting 0.3 % and 1.3 % GDP growth in 2013 and 2014, respectively (Nordea, 2013). With almost 4 years slowing growth, the Danish economy was expected to have an uptick in growth driven by rising domestic demand, higher consumer spending, and mounting investment activity. However, the waning activity in neighboring German, Swedish, and British markets also put Danish exports under pressure (Nordea, 2013).

In Finland, the economy was weakened by the lack of both international and domestic demands, with no increase in 2013. Foreign trade volumes and investment were also expected to fall in 2013. The labor market may deteriorate through 2013 with stagnant household purchasing power. Real GDP growth was projected to be −0.5 % in 2013, down from −0.2 % in 2012. However, from the end of 2013 to 2014, exports were expected to recover following a pickup in the world trade volumes and investment. In addition, private consumption will increase with projected real GDP growth of 1.5 % (Nordea, 2013).

According to OECD (Gecodia, 2013) Iceland has gradually recovered from its financial meltdown, with real GDP growth improving from −3.2 % in 2010 to 2.2 % and 2.9 % in 2011 and 2012, respectively. Similarly, private consumption increased from 0.2 % in 2010 to 2.9 % and 2.7 % in 2011 and 2012, respectively. Its net lending percentage GDP decreased from −7.8 % in 2010 to −2.7 % and −1.4 % in 2011 and 2012, respectively. IMF estimated its real GDP growth will be 2.7 %, 2.7 %, and 3.0 % in 2013, 2014, and 2015, respectively (Gecodia, 2013). Unemployment is forecasted to fall slightly below the structural rate of around 5 % by 2014 (OECD, 2013). In general, Iceland has gradually put the 2008 financial nightmare behind itself with a steady recovery.

Norway is expected to have sliding real GDP growth, from 3.4 % in 2012 to 2.6 % in 2013 and 2.2 % in 2014 (Nordea, 2013). Unemployment has increased and wage growth was lower than expected in 2013. In general, Norway's growth outlook was expected to be weak until late 2014 (Nordea, 2013).

Sweden experienced a slight 0.7 % real GDP growth in 2012; however, growth was expected to be 1.5 % and 2.5 % for 2013 and 2014, respectively (Nordea, 2013). Private consumption, rising wages, low inflation, and tax cuts were main driving forces of the predicted growth. However, unemployment in Sweden remains high.

The next chapter will give a brief background and qualitative analysis of the financial crisis as it relates to these five Nordic countries as a whole and individually.

Chapter 2
Impact of the 2008 Global Financial Crisis

The 2008 global financial crisis originated in the financial markets before gradually spilling over into the real economy through confidence fallout, capital outflows, reducing consumption, and decreasing export demands. It was rooted in the interplay of weaknesses in financial markets and macroeconomic imbalances in the international economy. As a result, many international banks needed financial support to survive or to maintain normal lending activity. In the Nordic countries it was primarily Icelandic banks that had operated with high risk, thus affecting its neighboring countries as well as the United Kingdom and the Netherlands to a greater degree. No country integrated into the global economy was left unaffected by this financial crisis; Nordic countries reported in this volume are therefore no exception.

To drive Europe's recovery, on November 26, 2008, the European Commission (Europa, 2008) announced a comprehensive Recovery Plan based on two mutually reinforcing elements: first, short-term measures to boost demand, save jobs, and help restore confidence, and second, longer-term "smart investment" to yield clean, energy-efficient higher growth and sustainable prosperity. The plan calls for a timely, targeted, and temporary fiscal stimulus of around US$256 billion (€200 billion based on 11/26/08 exchange rate) or 1.5 % of EU GDP, within both national budgets (around US$217.6 billion or €170 billion, 1.2 % of GDP) and EU and European Investment Bank budgets (around US$38.4 billion or €30 billion, 0.3 % of GDP).

With the early 1990s banking crisis experience and the ensuing persistent structural reforms, these Nordic countries were in a better position (except Iceland) at the onset of the 2008 global financial crisis. Yet, with relatively small economies and heavy reliance on exports, most of them are still hard-hit by this crisis. According to European Commission, Sweden's, Denmark's, and Finland's discretionary stimulus measures in 2009 and 2010 were in the range of 0.7–2.7 % of their GDP (Lindvall, 2011).

In order to present the impact of the 2008 global financial crisis, this chapter first graphically compares the overall economic development of the five countries during the time period from 2005 to 2010. Then, it elaborates on the financial crisis

C.Y.-Y. Lin et al., *National Intellectual Capital and the Financial Crisis in Denmark, Finland, Iceland, Norway, and Sweden*, SpringerBriefs in Economics,
DOI 10.1007/978-1-4614-9536-9_2, © The Author(s) 2014

impact on each country individually in the sequence of Denmark, Finland, Iceland, Norway, and Sweden.

The impact of the 2008 global financial crisis on each country can be easily observed from the following four graphs, namely, the percentage of real GDP growth per capita, total general government debt percentage of GDP, unemployment rate of labor force, and consumer price inflation.

Comparisons of the Five Economies

This section presents four graphs in order to examine these Nordic countries as a whole from 2005 to 2010. Figure 2.1 shows that the five countries had negative **real GDP growth** during the financial crisis (2008 and 2009), except Finland's 0.45 % positive growth in 2008. The sharp decline in 2009 reflects the impact of the financial crisis. The fast rebound of Denmark, Finland, and Sweden explains that these three countries had better recovery, comparing to Iceland and Norway. Among them, Norway had the least fluctuation during the crisis, very likely due to its stronger reserves from the oil revenues. Yet, in 2010 Norway's real GDP growth was still negative. For Iceland, the aftereffect of its financial breakdown needs more time to recover and its real GDP growth was also negative in 2010. Over the 6 years, the real GDP growth development pattern was somewhat similar in Denmark, Finland, and Sweden, with Sweden recovering the best after the financial crisis.

Figure 2.2 indicates the total **general government debt** percentage GDP of the five countries. The reason for reporting government debt is based on an academic research finding. After researching 800 years of financial crises, Reinhart and Rogoff (2009) commented that the overhang of public and private debt is the most important impediment to a normal recovery from recession.

Figure 2.2 indicates that Iceland had increasing government debt after 2007, due to its financial system breakdown. The other four countries largely had similar level of government debt before and after the financial crisis, with Sweden even reducing its debt a little and the other three countries increasing a little after the financial crisis. Yet, it is fair to say that Denmark, Finland, Norway, and Sweden all have sound financial systems that withstood the impact of this financial turmoil. In addition, their government debts were within the EU standard of below 60 % of GDP.

Figure 2.3 shows that all the countries had **unemployment rate** increases starting from 2009, except Norway. Iceland particularly had a drastic raise, due to its financial breakdown. Denmark started out with a much lower unemployment rate than Finland and Sweden; however, the gap narrowed after the financial crisis. Norway's unemployment rate was relatively stable over the 6 years. After the financial crisis, its 2010 rate was even lower than that of 2005, reflecting its successful measure in preserving job opportunities. The unemployment rate development patterns of Finland and Sweden are very similar and became almost

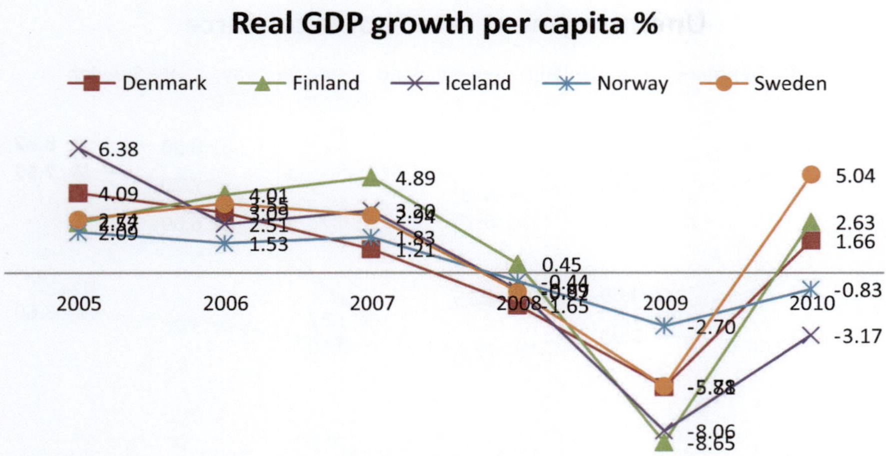

Fig. 2.1 Real GDP growth per capita of Denmark, Finland, Iceland, Norway, and Sweden from 2005 to 2010

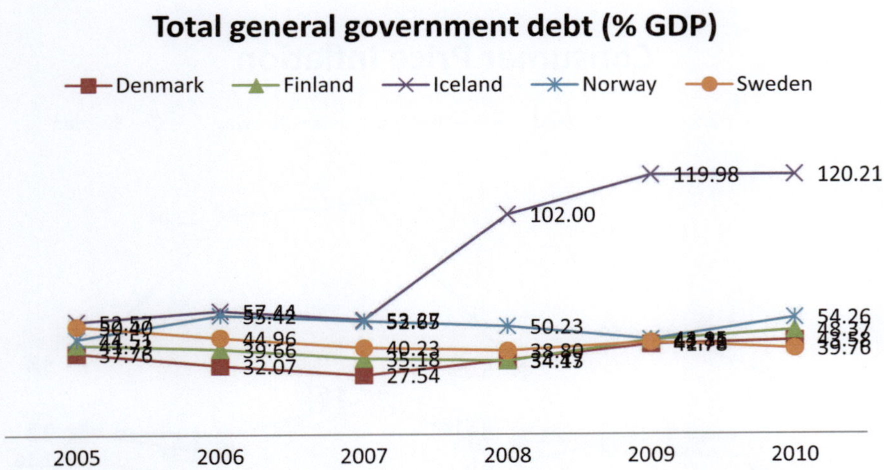

Fig. 2.2 Total general government debt (% GDP) of Denmark, Finland, Iceland, Norway, and Sweden from 2005 to 2010

identical in the last 3 years. When comparing the rate in 2005 and 2010, Finland remained the same, Norway had a reduction, and the other three countries all had an increase.

Figure 2.4 shows the **consumer price inflation** of the five countries. Iceland had a hike in inflation in 2008 and 2009, yet it reduced sharply in 2010. The development pattern of consumer price inflation (CPI) is similar for the other four countries, with gradual increase from 2005 to 2008 and then an obvious decrease in 2009, very

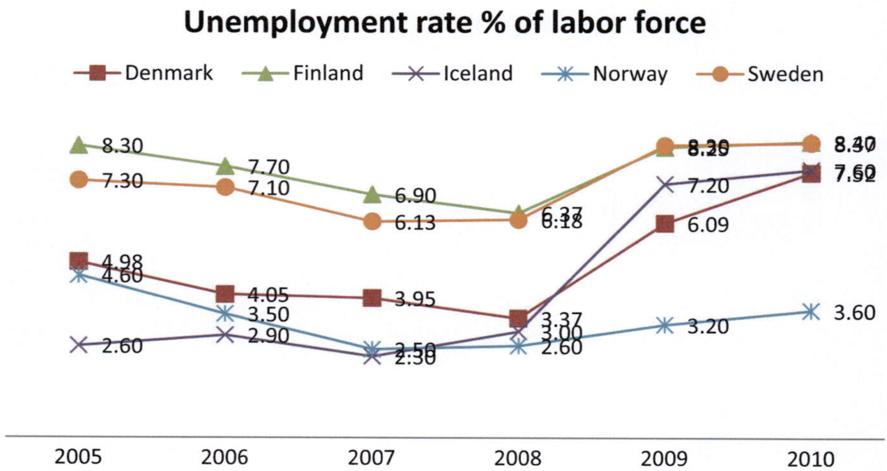

Fig. 2.3 Unemployment rate of Denmark, Finland, Iceland, Norway, and Sweden from 2005 to 2010

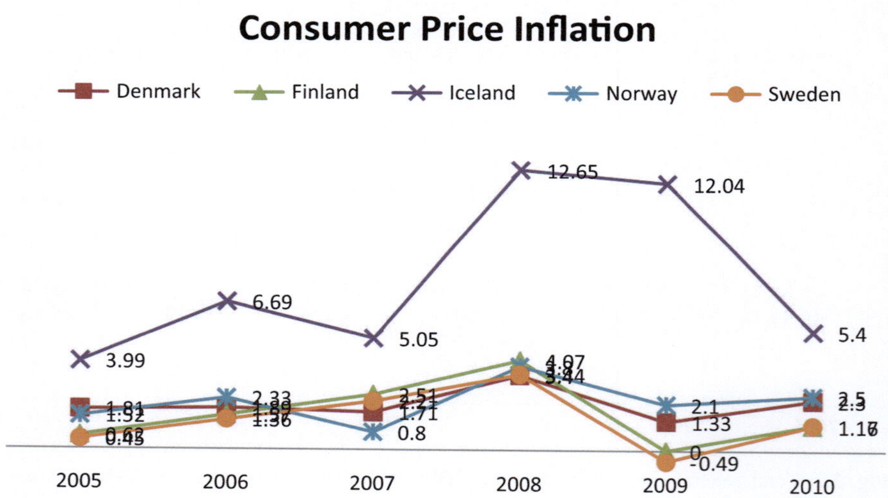

Fig. 2.4 Consumer price inflation of Denmark, Finland, Iceland, Norway, and Sweden from 2005 to 2010

likely because of the effect of the stimulus package. When comparing the CPI in 2005 and 2010, Iceland increases a little and the other four countries had a similar level at the beginning and end of the financial crisis.

In general, the above four figures for the five countries indicate that real GDP growth per capital, unemployment rate, and consumer price inflation show the impact of the 2008 global financial crisis. The total general government debt remained relatively stable, except in Iceland. Interestingly, the development patterns of Denmark, Finland, and Sweden for the presented four indicators are pretty similar. These three countries are also the countries that suffered the most during the early 1990s Nordic banking crisis. Apparently, they have learned their lesson and follow more prudent financial regulations, hence the similar financial status. Iceland unfortunately experienced a financial system breakdown and had a very different profile from the other countries. Norway has its own distinctive pattern, as it enjoys the high petroleum revenues and had more leeway during the financial crisis. In general, these four figures show that the 2008 financial crisis did exert some impact on these countries' economic development, yet it was not as serious as expected and their recovery was obvious, except Iceland.

In what follows, we briefly describe the impact of the 2008 global financial crisis on these five Nordic countries. The depth of the report depends on the English literature available for each country. For readers to gain a general picture about the efforts that each country has put in to mitigating the negative impact of the financial crisis, we have summarized the details of stimulus packages implemented by these countries in Appendix 1. Please note that the reported package is based on publicly available data and is not an exhaustive list. In addition, the reported amounts of stimulus packages were based on the exchange rate at the time of each stimulus and thus vary. Readers can also refer to Appendix 2 for the important meetings conducted by key global leaders during this financial crisis.

Denmark

Denmark is a country highly dependent on foreign trade with a modern market economy that features a high-tech agricultural sector, state-of-the-art industry with world-leading firms in pharmaceuticals, maritime shipping, and renewable energy (Central Intelligence Agency [CIA], 2011). The Danish economy did not escape the global financial and economic crisis (OECD, 2009), primarily due to mismanagement and lax credit policies resulting in an enormous deposit deficit that became impossible to finance after the interbank money market froze (Carstensen, 2011). Before the crisis, the Danish economy was already overheated through an explosion in housing prices from 2005 to 2007, with real GNP in Denmark falling dramatically (Carstensen, 2011). The deterioration in financial conditions and collapse of world trade, along with the ending of the property boom, hit Denmark hard. Danish GDP was cut by 0.9 % in 2008 and 5.2 % in 2009, although it did not fall as much as in some neighboring countries. The historically low levels of unemployment rose sharply with the recession but remain about half the level of the EU (CIA, 2011). Nevertheless, Denmark entered the recession with a strong fiscal position and a sound fiscal policy framework (CIA, 2011; OECD, 2009). In addition, large budget surpluses have reduced debt, and the government had a positive net asset position of about 5 % of its GDP in 2008 (OECD). These favorable conditions had helped the country weather through the crisis.

The strength of the Danish system is its transparency and low origination costs. For instance, compared to the US subprime problem, Danish mortgage bonds were a liability of the mortgage bank issuing it and were supported by the capital, reserves, and income of the bank as well as by the mortgage loans that collateralize that particular bond. If the collateral happened to suffer large losses, the bond holders were protected by the entire resources of the bank (The Mortgage Professor, 2009). Therefore, its mortgage bond market continued to function during the financial crisis. Although the system experienced some stress, it was much less affected by the subprime outbreak (OECD, 2009).

To deal with the crisis, financial sector policy measures in Denmark were extensive. The measures taken by the Danish state were focused on two overall challenges: sustain financial stability to keep the financial system afloat and keep the financial crisis from causing too much turmoil in the real economy (Carstensen, 2011). A range of temporary measures were taken by the central bank to provide liquidity and credibility to the Danish financial system, such as creating temporary credit facilities, offering an expansion of the collateral base, and creating an option to obtain credit on the basis of excess capital adequacy. Among various measures, two important bailout bank packages (Bank Package I and II) were implemented (Carstensen, 2011). Bank Package I, presented on October 5, 2008, issued a 2-year state guarantee of all deposits (exclusive of covered bonds and mortgage credit bonds), with the state's support of US$777 billion (DKK 4,200 billion) in deposits. On January 18, 2009, Bank Package II was launched to ensure normal lending activity by banks. Specifically, Danish government offered a hybrid capital totaling US$17.8 billion (DKK 100 billion) to its banks and mortgage banks (Kredittilsynet, 2009). Thus, the liquidity measures were strengthened by prolonging the government guarantee scheme on deposits to 2013. The package also strengthened regulation and supervision and entrusted the Danish Financial Supervisory Authority (FSA) to conduct at least a yearly review of institutions' solvency needs so that their needs and risks can be made public (Kredittilsynet, 2009).

The creation of the bailout fund by the government and the Danish banking sector serves to guarantee all claims of unsecured creditors on participating banks (OECD, 2009). The regulatory resources to supervise medium- and smaller-sized institutions have also been increased. Particularly, fiscal targets are set according to a medium-term framework based on fiscal sustainability assessments. In addition to increased government investment spending, the previously decided tax cuts took effect in 2009. A major tax reform package was legislated in early 2009, aimed at raising labor supply and reducing the government financing gap in the long run but providing demand stimulus in the short run. The release of funds from the compulsory private Special Pension scheme significantly eased households' liquidity constraints (OECD, 2009).

Furthermore, on October 27, 2008, Denmark's National Bank and the European Central Bank established an equivalent swap line for 12 billion Euro (Bernstein, 2010). The swap facility was very helpful in addressing the banks' liquidity needs.

Without negative effect on the foreign exchange reserve, it supported the Danish krone indirectly by calming and sending a strong positive signal to the market. In November and December 2008, the Danish government took another step in issuing 30-year bonds; thus, Danish pension funds restructured their portfolios from foreign to domestic securities (Bernstein, 2010). These measures contributed strongly to keeping capital outflows at a manageable level during the crisis and stabilized the Danish economy.

Finland

Finland has made a remarkable transformation from a farm and forest economy to a diversified modern, open, highly industrialized, and free-market economy with vibrant information and communication technology sectors (CIA, 2011; Heritage Foundation, 2012). In the twenty-first century, the key features of its modern welfare state are a high standard of education, equality promotion, and national social security system. Finland has been one of the best performing economies within the EU over the past decade. It is also renowned as one of the innovation powerhouses in Europe (Palkamo, 2011). In recent years, trade has become more and more important with exports accounting for over one-third of its GDP.

Despite the fact that Finland was insulated from the direct effects of the recent global financial crisis due to its prudently managed financial sector, the worldwide recession and the collapse in trade hit this small and export-driven country harder than most other OECD countries (CIA, 2011; OECD, 2010; Tervanen, 2009). Real GDP declined by over 9 % from the peak in mid-2008 to the second quarter of 2009, led by declining export volumes of almost one-third. This collapse in trade can to a large extent be attributed to Finland's high dependence on information and communication technology (ICT) and capital goods exports, and its exceptional exposure to hard-hit markets such as Russia (OECD, 2010).

Finland's financial system is highly internationalized and is vulnerable to the deterioration in global financial markets. Nonresident investment owns about 80 % of the publicly traded companies, and about one-quarter of the businesses is invested by nonresidents (Lin, 2009). In addition, a majority of the large companies in Finland are multinational corporations. For instance, with deep involvement in Icelandic banks, the breakdown of Icelandic financial system affected Finland greatly. The takeover of the three largest Icelandic banks by the Icelandic government was also reflected in the Finnish branches of these banks. After Icelandic Kaupthing Bank suspended operations of its Finnish branch in October 2008, the Finnish government provided a state guarantee against the legal risks incurred by the parties taking part in the arrangement. Yet, this approach differs from the solution adopted in other EU countries, because it provides for a more rapid and convenient recovery for depositors (Tervanen, 2009).

To revive the economy, the Finnish discretionary stimulus measures were similar in size to the expansionary packages that were adopted in other Nordic countries, amounting to 1.7 % of GDP in 2009 (IceNews, 2009). The composition of the package included 40 % of the measures represented tax cuts and the abolition of employers' national insurance contributions; approximately 20 % were categorized as construction, renovation, and civil engineering; 2 % went to labor policy and education; and 3 % went to benefit increases (Lindvall, 2011). These priorities are consistent with the agenda of the government and with the economic model that Finnish government has built after the deep recession of the early 1990s. A large portion of the taxes collected at the central level are transferred to local governments and social security funds; consequently, local governments have a lot of autonomy and play a large role in public service delivery (OECD, 2011a). Therefore, for successful implementation, the local governments need to take their share of the responsibility.

Iceland

Prior to the 2008 crisis, Iceland had achieved high growth, low unemployment, and a remarkably even distribution of income. Literacy, longevity, and social cohesion are first rate by world standards. The economy depends heavily on the fishing industry, which provides 40 % of export earnings, more than 12 % of its GDP, and employs 7 % of the workforce (CIA, 2011). In the last decade, Iceland's economy has been diversifying into manufacturing and service industries, particularly within the fields of software production, biotechnology, and tourism. In 2007, the Icelandic government had a relatively healthy balance, with sovereign debt at 28 % of its GDP and a budget surplus of 6 % of its GDP. Much of Iceland's economic growth in recent years came as the result of a boom in domestic demand following the rapid expansion of the country's financial sector after the privatization of the banking sector in the early 2000s.

The growth in the banking sector laid the basis for substantial macroeconomic imbalances. At the end of 2007, household debt measured close to 220 % of disposable income, of which 80 % was indexed to domestic price levels, while around 10 % was denominated in foreign currency (Kredittilsynet, 2009). Household borrowing was mainly channeled into the housing market and to consumption, contributing to an overheated housing market and high inflation. The corporate sector also showed a substantial debt buildup in the period. Nonfinancial firms' debt measured over 300 % of its GDP in 2007. Icelandic banks accounted for about two-thirds of these loans, which were mainly denominated in foreign currency (Kredittilsynet, 2009).

The aggressive expansion of Icelandic domestic banks in foreign markets and heavy borrowing by consumers and businesses in foreign currencies caused the buildup of considerable systemic risk for such a small economy (Economic Freedom, 2011). Worsening global financial conditions throughout 2008 resulted in a sharp depreciation of the Icelandic currency krona vis-à-vis other major currencies. As a result, Iceland's financial sector was severely affected by the global financial turmoil. The foreign exposure of Icelandic banks, whose loans and other assets totaled more than 10 times the country's GDP, became unsustainable (CIA, 2011).

At the end of the second quarter of 2008, the Icelandic stock exchange had dropped by more than 90 %. Inflation soared to 13.9 % in the third quarter of 2008 from 3.8 % one year earlier (Carey, 2009). Since October 2008, 14 % of the workforce had experienced reductions in pay, and around 7 % had had their working hours reduced. Iceland's three largest banks collapsed in late 2008. The general government budget balance (excluding debt write-offs) plunged from near balance in 2008 to a deficit of 10 % of its GDP. Total direct fiscal cost was about 20 % of its GDP, which is higher than in any other country except Ireland (OECD, 2011b).

Since the collapse of Iceland's financial sector, government economic priorities have included stabilizing the krona, reducing Iceland's high budget deficit, containing inflation, restructuring the financial sector, and diversifying the economy (CIA, 2011). During the crisis, Iceland had been able to secure over US$10 billion in loans from the International Monetary Fund (IMF) and other countries to stabilize its currency and financial sector, and to back government guarantees for foreign deposits in Icelandic banks (CIA). Since around US$1,285 million (£840 million) in cash from more than 100 United Kingdom (UK) local authorities was invested in Icelandic banks (BBC, 2008), negotiation was settled that up to 4 % of Iceland's gross domestic product (GDP) will be paid to the UK from 2017 to 2023. In addition, the similarly involved Netherlands will receive up to 2 % of Iceland's GDP for the same period (Valdimarsson, 2009).

On Oct. 14, 2008, the Central Bank of Iceland drew on its swap facilities with the central banks of Denmark and Norway for around US$273 million (€200 million) each. Iceland has swap facilities with the other Nordic countries for a total of around US$2 billion (€1.5 billion) (Central Bank of Iceland [CBI], 2008). It was also seeking assistance from the European Central Bank (ECB) (Kennedy, 2008). The IMF-led package of US$4.6 billion was finally agreed on November 19, 2008, with the IMF loaning US$2.1 billion and another US$2.5 billion of loans and currency swaps from Norway, Sweden, Finland, and Denmark. In addition, Poland offered to lend US$200 million and the Faroe Islands offered US$50 million, about 3 % of Faroese GDP (Brogger & Einarsdottir, 2008). The Icelandic Prime Minister's Office also reported that Russia offered US$300 million. Later, Germany, the Netherlands, and the UK also announced a joint loan of US$6.3 billion (€5 billion), related to the deposit insurance dispute (Dutch News, 2008; Mason, 2008).

From the above report, it is clear that the world organization, such as IMF, plays a very important role in stabilizing the world economy. Countries mentioned also offered timely assistance to help Iceland combat its financial turmoil.

Norway

The Norwegian economy features a combination of free-market activity and government intervention. Norway is highly dependent on the petroleum sector, which increased its share to 28 % of its GDP in 2008 due to high oil prices (CIA, 2011). The value of exports accounted for 48 % of its GDP in 2008, while that of imports accounted for 28.9 % of its GDP (Norwegian Confederation of Trade Union, 2010). Being a small and open economy with free movement of capital, the negative effects of international financial troubles were rapidly reflected in the dollar-based Norwegian interbank market. When the dollar market completely dried up in the wake of the Lehman Brothers' failure, it became difficult for Norwegian banks to obtain funding (Kredittilsynet, 2009).

The turmoil spread quickly to Norway. Oslo Børs stock market dropped as much as 54 % in 2008 (Kredittilsynet, 2009). Private consumption in particular fell sharply. In the fourth quarter of 2008 and the first quarter of 2009, Norway experienced negative GDP growth, but growth picked up slightly again in the second quarter of 2009 (Halvorsen, 2009). Unemployment rose far less than in most other countries and was just above 3 %. Compared to many countries, Norway managed the 2008 financial crisis relatively well.

Yet, its government adopted the most ambitious fiscal policy measures in more than 30 years when compared with other countries (Halvorsen, 2009; Juel, 2011; Kredittilsynet, 2009). The stimulus package entails an overall budget impulse of 2.3 % of Norway's mainland (non-oil) GDP (Kredittilsynet). The use of petroleum revenues, as measured by the structural, non-oil budget deficit, was estimated to be around US$20.8 billion (NOK 130 billion), reflecting the authorities' large financial room for maneuvering (Juel, 2011). Extensive measures to stabilize the financial markets were established, which improved Norwegian banks' access to liquidity and long-term funding, and strengthened individual banks' ability to uphold lending activity to households and businesses (Halvorsen, 2009).

On October 12, 2008, the government presented a package to give banks better access to liquidity and financing, thus to calm and provide confidence in the financial market. For example, with a limit of around US$56 billion (NOK 350 billion), the government would give banks access to collateral that could facilitate new long-term borrowing; the banks could also exchange preferential bonds for government securities (Kredittilsynet, 2009). In addition, the Norwegian Guarantee Institute for Export Credits (GIEK) was authorized to issue new loan commitments up to a limit of around US$12.8 billion (NOK 80 billion) for the "general guarantee arrangement" and around US$1.04 billion (NOK 6.5 billion) for the "construction loan arrangement" for constructing ships. In the fiscal budget for 2009, the government entailed a fiscal policy stimulus of around US$3.2 billion (NOK 20 billion), breaking down to around 16 % in tax relief and 84 % in increased public spending, distributed across local and central government authorities (Kredittilsynet, 2009). The government also gave special priority to local authorities and transport projects, allocating around US$1.02 million (NOK 6.4 million) and US$0.61 billion (NOK 3.8 billion), respectively (Kredittilsynet, 2009).

Norway's financial package was presented on February 8, 2009, to assure credit supply to households and firms and to stabilize the financial market. In addition, the government established two new funds with a total capital of around US$16 billion (NOK 100 billion). The Government Finance Fund supplied up to US$8 billion

(NOK 50 billion) of capital to banks, which enabled banks to maintain normal lending activities. The Government Bond Fund (GBF), managed by the National Insurance Scheme Fund, was a temporary fund capped at US$8 billion (NOK 50 billion) that invested in Norwegian bonds. Together with other investors, the GBF purchased ordinary bonds issued by Norwegian firms in both the primary and secondary markets (Kredittilsynet, 2009). Kredittilsynet (the Financial Supervisory Authority of Norway) particularly encouraged the banks to make use of the instruments offered by the Government Finance Fund to assure sound capital adequacy and a robust basis to meet households' and firms' credit needs (Kredittilsynet). However, only small fractions of the capital allocated to the two funds were used as the capital market quickly recovered and functioned better during the spring of 2009 than expected (Juel, 2011). Readers can refer to Appendix 1 for the details of the stimulus package.

In addition to the above stated stimulus package, other measures also help revive the Norwegian economy. The introduction of a "swap scheme" along with a more flexible liquidity supply to Norwegian banks gradually brought a significant improvement in the functioning of the short-term money market. Extending the duration of "swap loans" from 3 to 5 years was also important in providing security (Kredittilsynet, 2009).

Furthermore, Norway's exports mainly consist of commodities, semifinished goods and equipment for offshore oil and gas exploration, and such demands did not collapse as machinery for manufacturing, trucks, and other vehicles did. Moreover, the price collapse in the commodities markets was avoided mainly due to China's continued strong economic growth, as China was using about 50 % of the world's metal production and about 10 % of world consumption of oil (Juel, 2011).

Another contributor was Norway's relatively large public sector, which helped stabilize the economy in turbulent times for it employs one-third of the labor force in Norway. These jobs were not directly threatened by the crisis, and the continued requirement for pensions, health care, and education ensures that the supply of these services was protected from the market turmoil (Halvorsen, 2009).

In summary, Norway's high oil revenues and reserves certainly contained the total effect on the Norwegian economy and resulted in a quick turnaround. Yet, its financial solidity was the result of decadelong fiscal discipline that the government's revenue from the petroleum sector should be accumulated in a sovereign wealth fund, and only the fund's estimated real return can be used in the annual budgets (Juel, 2011). Such discipline contributed to the reserves that can be maneuvered during the bad times.

Sweden

Sweden is a small and open economy with extensive foreign trade and a financial market that is well integrated with the international markets. Aided by peace and neutrality in the twentieth century, Sweden has achieved an enviable standard of living under a mixed system of high-tech capitalism and extensive welfare benefits. Sweden has a modern distribution system, excellent internal and external communications, and a skilled labor force (CIA, 2011). Its banking regulations and lending practices are prudent and sensible after the early 1990s banking crisis. Monetary stability is well maintained, with inflationary pressures under control.

Over time, Sweden's dependence on the outside world has increased. The proportion of its exports increased from just over 20 % in 1990 to around 40 % in 2007 (Oberg, 2009), and total trade accounted for more than 50 % of its GDP (Economic Freedom, 2011). This means that an international economic downturn and a decline in export demand would have serious consequences for the production and employment in Sweden. In addition, the market funding rather than deposits accounted for around 60 % of the banks' total balance sheets and was acquired on international markets (Oberg, 2009).

Despite strong finances and fundamentals, the Swedish economy slid into recession in the third quarter of 2008, and growth continued downward in 2009 as deteriorating global conditions reduced export demand and consumption (CIA, 2011). Beginning in the last quarter of 2008, the Swedish manufacturing industry was affected most sharply (Jochem, 2010). Yet, Sweden's prudent fiscal management in the years prior to the global economic turmoil created fiscal space for some stimulus measures, including labor market support and social security tax cuts (Economic Freedom, 2011). Aggressive interest rates cuts, unconventional policy measures, and exceptional government support to the financial system all helped contain the length and depth of the recession (Gurria, 2011).

Drawing on lessons learned in the early 1990s banking crisis, the Swedish government has actively intervened in the financial system (Jochem, 2010). A Swedish stabilization plan was adopted on October 29, 2008. Policies aimed at stabilizing the economy were mostly integrated into the budgetary process (Jochem, 2010). In general, Sweden's approach to crisis management has been a mix of spending on infrastructure and public employment on the one side and tax or fiscal policies aimed at stimulating business and private consumption on the other. Two-thirds of these measures were related to tax cuts. The corporate income tax rate was reduced from 28 % to 26.3 % (0.21 % of GDP). Additionally, the general employers' contribution rate was reduced from 32.42 % to 31.42 % (0.22 % of its GDP) (Jochem, 2010). The basic tax deduction was raised for people aged 65 or above (0.05 % of its GDP), and employers' contribution rebate for youth employees was enlarged (0.02 % of its GDP). Furthermore, the government increased spending in a variety of sectors such as infrastructure, education, and social security. The largest item was a rise in transport infrastructure spending (0.11 % of GDP) (Jochem, 2010).

The plan also covered a guarantee program of up to US$210 billion (SEK 1,500 billion) to support banks' and building societies' medium-term financing. A stability fund of around US$2.1 billion (SEK 15 billion) was set up in preparing for future solvency problems at Swedish financial institutions. However, banks participating in the guarantee scheme were subject to curbs on executive pay, bonus, and termination compensation payments for management in the period of the guarantee agreement. Further, on December 5, 2008, the Swedish government presented a fiscal policy package worth around US$1.2 billion (SEK 8.3 billion), providing an overall fiscal stimulus equivalent to 1.3 % of its GDP. A rescue package for the car industry worth around US$3.9 billion (SEK 28 billion) was presented on December 11, 2008. At the start of 2009, a package was also offered for the recapitalization of Swedish banks, and the Riksbank (Swedish National Debt Office) provided a guarantee in respect of bank debt (Kredittilsynet, 2009). Most of the stimulus was spread over a period from 2009 until 2011 and approximately one-third of the total measures are explicitly temporary (Jochem, 2010). Readers can refer to Appendix 1 for the details of the stimulus package.

In addition to the stimulus package, the Riksbank and the US Federal Reserve set up temporary reciprocal swap facilities worth a total of US$30 billion. A separate swap facility was established with the European Central Bank as well. Another stabilizing force is that the Swedish state employed over 28 % of the total labor force in 2005 (Jochem, 2010), which was not affected too much by the financial crisis.

Another important reason that enabled the Swedish economy to enter the global recession in a sound position was its strict rules for financial policy making. Since 1997, the Swedish government has been required to present a medium-term fiscal framework as policy projections. Sweden has also benefited from some valuable lessons learned during a similar, but local, financial crisis in the early 1990s (Freden, 2008; Jochem, 2010). Particularly, Freden (2008) mentioned one priceless asset: the Swedes trust their governments, regardless of political color, to stick to basically the same steady economic course. Since growth has been quite high for more than a decade, inflation has been kept low, and the public finances kept under control, most Swedes are confident in the future. Therefore, they did not hesitate to invest, employ, or consume once the recession bottomed out, and the crisis therefore blew over faster in Sweden than in many other countries (Freden).

In the face of the crisis, Sweden's healthy public finances and strong economic fundamentals proved a major asset. Owing to the solid public finances and a strong fiscal framework, the country has had considerable maneuvering room with which to counteract the economic downturn, and thus it weathered the 2008 global financial and economic crisis well.

Chapter 3
National Intellectual Capital Development of the Five Nordic Countries

In this chapter, we first present the development of national intellectual capital (NIC) in the five Nordic countries over the 6-year time frame and then graphically display the relationships between each individual component of NIC with GDP per capita (ppp). Afterward, we describe the relative positions of long-term and short-term intellectual capital in these five countries and explain the dynamics of NIC for three time periods (2005–2006, 2007–2008, and 2009–2010). Finally, we illustrate the NIC trajectory of these five countries on three-dimensional (3D) 48-country landscapes.

National Intellectual Capital Development

The NIC measurement model in this study is based upon the indicators described in Appendix 3, containing human capital, market capital, process capital, renewal capital, and financial capital. This model has been statistically proven for its validity and reliability. The definitions of the indicators are listed in Appendix 4. This booklet series covers a total of 48 countries in 11 country clusters (see Appendix 5 for details).

For a full picture of all 48 countries, Appendix 6 exhibits the scores and rankings of human capital, market capital, process capital, renewal capital, financial capital, and overall NIC covered in this booklet series. Table 3.1 summarizes the status of these five countries compared with the total 48 countries reported in Appendix 6. Appendix 7 provides the individual economic profiles with additional statistics. For the NIC ranking, Sweden ranks 1, followed by Denmark at 3, Finland at 4, Iceland at 8, and Norway at 9. All of them are among the top ten ranking countries, and Denmark, Finland, and Sweden are among the top five. The ranking is consistent with the general perception that the Nordic countries are advanced countries with both good tangible and intangible assets.

From Table 3.1, Denmark excels in human capital (#1) and process capital (#1), Finland performs well in process capital (#3) and renewal capital (#3), Norway is at

C.Y.-Y. Lin et al., *National Intellectual Capital and the Financial Crisis in Denmark, Finland, Iceland, Norway, and Sweden*, SpringerBriefs in Economics,
DOI 10.1007/978-1-4614-9536-9_3,

Table 3.1 National intellectual capital ranking of Denmark, Finland, Iceland, Norway, and Sweden (2005–2010)

	Human capital		Market capital		Process capital		Renewal capital		Financial capital		NIC	
Country	Score	Ranking	Score	Ranking	Score	Ranking	Score	Ranking	Score	Ranking	Score	Ranking
Denmark	8.545	1	6.662	6	7.642	1	6.587	6	9.665	13	39.101	3
Finland	7.601	9	6.232	10	7.399	3	7.755	3	9.606	17	38.593	4
Iceland	8.357	3	5.614	21	6.561	12	5.931	8	9.713	8	36.154	8
Norway	7.936	5	6.055	14	7.008	7	4.961	15	9.987	1	35.947	9
Sweden	8.385	2	6.563	7	7.174	6	7.780	2	9.673	12	39.575	1

the top in financial capital (#1), and Sweden is high in both human capital (#2) and renewal capital (#2).

The following six figures compare human capital, market capital, process capital, renewal capital, financial capital, and NIC for the five countries. All individual capital scores are based on a 1–10 scale with the NIC score being the sum of the five capital scores. Please note that our data source – IMD Competitiveness Yearbook – did not report Iceland's 2007 and 2008 data, due to its financial system breakdown. We connected Iceland's vacant years with dotted line to show the sharp drop of some capitals.

Human Capital

National human capital represents a nation's investment in nurturing qualified human resources, such as higher education enrollment, skilled labor, and public expenditure in education. Human capital is a long-term-oriented NIC (Lin & Edvinsson, 2011, p. 323), which takes time to develop and is not susceptible to external impact. Figure 3.1 shows that human capital of these five countries was rather stable and their relative position largely remains the same over the 6 years. Comparing the scores of 2005 and 2010, Iceland's human capital scored higher in 2010 than 2005, but the other four countries had a score decrease.

Market Capital

National market capital represents international trade and relationships such as cross-border ventures, globalization, and exports of goods. Figure 3.2 shows that market capital of the five countries is close to each other in 2005, yet separated into two groups in 2010 with Iceland dropping drastically after the financial crisis. Iceland's data for 2007 and 2008 is missing; therefore, we connected the vacant years with a dotted line. When comparing the score of 2010 with that of 2005, Denmark, Finland, and Iceland had market capital decreases, and Norway had exactly the same score. Sweden advanced its last position in 2005 to the first position in 2010 among the five countries, showing continuous progress in market capital with a small score decrease in 2009 only.

Process Capital

National process capital represents the infrastructure required for building a prosperous society, such as capital availability, mobile phone subscribers, and government efficiency. Figure 3.3 shows that when comparing the score of 2010 with that

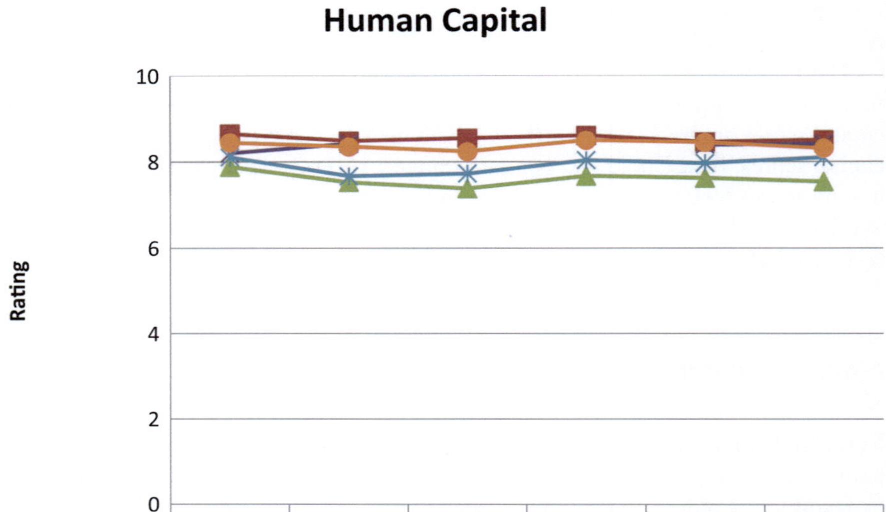

	2005	2006	2007	2008	2009	2010
Denmark	8.65	8.49	8.55	8.61	8.46	8.51
Finland	7.88	7.52	7.38	7.67	7.62	7.53
Iceland	8.20	8.42			8.39	8.42
Norway	8.11	7.67	7.73	8.04	7.97	8.10
Sweden	8.45	8.35	8.24	8.50	8.45	8.31

Fig. 3.1 Human capital of Denmark, Finland, Iceland, Norway, and Sweden

of 2005, all the countries had a process capital decrease, except Sweden which increased over the years. Again, Iceland had a relatively large-scale score decrease and its vacant years of missing values are connected with a dotted line.

Renewal Capital

National renewal capital represents the capability of R&D and innovation, such as R&D spending, scientific articles, and patents. Different from the previous three graphs, Fig. 3.4 shows a wider gap among the countries. In 2005, there are three distinctive groups, with Finland and Sweden in the top group, Denmark and Iceland the middle group, and Norway by itself the low group. In 2010, renewal capital evolved into two groups. Denmark, Finland, and Sweden were grouped together with Denmark's progression and Finland's and Sweden's small regression. Iceland and Norway became a group in 2010, with Iceland's regression and Norway's slight progression. Sweden used to enjoy a high level of renewal capital, so its regression

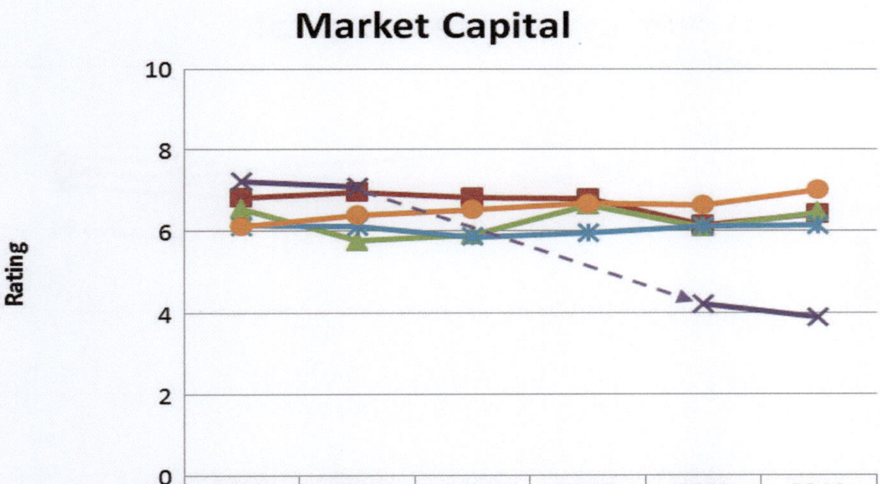

	2005	2006	2007	2008	2009	2010
Denmark	6.83	6.96	6.81	6.81	6.15	6.42
Finland	6.56	5.76	5.91	6.63	6.09	6.45
Iceland	7.23	7.10			4.22	3.90
Norway	6.14	6.13	5.86	5.96	6.11	6.14
Sweden	6.12	6.40	6.51	6.68	6.63	7.03

Fig. 3.2 Market capital of Denmark, Finland, Iceland, Norway, and Sweden

in 2010 may have some implications for further pursuit. In addition, Norway's persistent low renewal capital among the Nordic countries deserves some attention.

Financial Capital

Financial capital is representative of GDP per capita (ppp) in US dollars transformed to a score on a scale of 1–10. The process of score transformation is explained in Appendix 3. Figure 3.5 shows that Norway is persistently the leading country in financial capital, for its high petroleum income. However, all the countries had a little score decrease in 2010, when compared with that in 2005. In real dollars, the average GDP per capita (ppp) of 2005–2010 is US$35,959 for Denmark, US$33,761 for Finland, US$37,923 for Iceland, US$51,035 for Norway, and US$36,305 for Sweden.

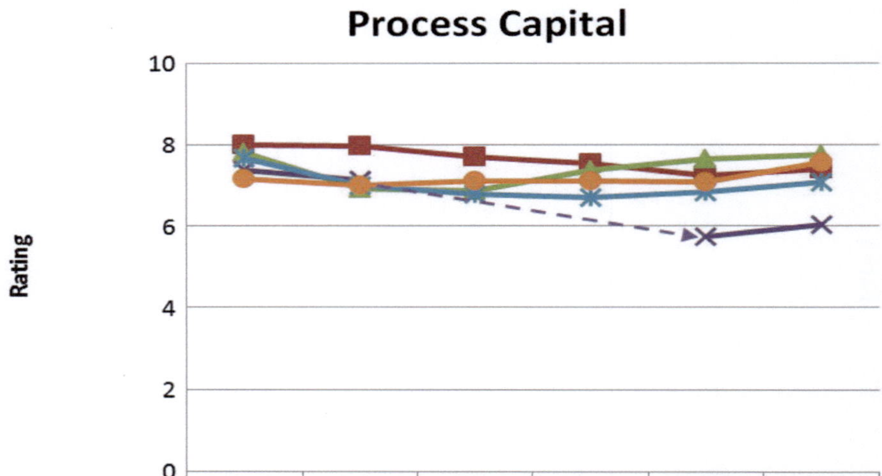

	2005	2006	2007	2008	2009	2010
Denmark	8.00	7.97	7.70	7.54	7.24	7.40
Finland	7.81	6.93	6.87	7.39	7.63	7.76
Iceland	7.38	7.13			5.72	6.02
Norway	7.66	6.99	6.79	6.70	6.84	7.07
Sweden	7.17	7.01	7.10	7.12	7.09	7.56

Fig. 3.3 Process capital of Denmark, Finland, Iceland, Norway, and Sweden

NIC

NIC is the overall national intellectual capital comprised of the five types of capital described above. Figure 3.6 presents the trends of overall NIC over the 6 years. In general, there is not much difference (except Iceland) over the 6 years spanning 2005–2010, meaning their valuable intangible assets were not affected too much by the financial crisis. When comparing NIC scores of 2005 and 2010, Denmark, Finland, and Norway had a little decrease; Iceland had a more obvious decrease, mainly because of its deep financial trouble; and Sweden had a little increase.

In 2005, the NIC of Norway was by itself with that of the other four countries clustered together as a group. Over the 5 years, Iceland dropped out of the group with its NIC score lower than Norway. The other three countries progressed together over the years. Norway still had some distance from Denmark, Finland, and Sweden in terms of national intellectual capital. In an era with increasing importance of intangible assets, this graph sends meaningful message for the Norwegian policy makers.

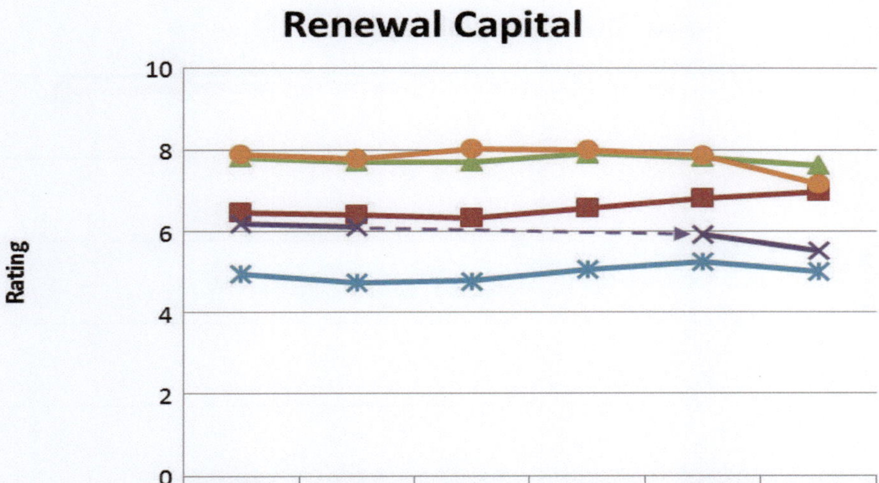

	2005	2006	2007	2008	2009	2010
Denmark	6.45	6.41	6.33	6.56	6.81	6.96
Finland	7.80	7.69	7.70	7.90	7.82	7.63
Iceland	6.18	6.10			5.91	5.53
Norway	4.96	4.73	4.77	5.05	5.26	5.00
Sweden	7.89	7.77	8.02	7.99	7.85	7.16

Fig. 3.4 Renewal capital of Denmark, Finland, Iceland, Norway, and Sweden

Relationship Between Each Individual Capital with GDP Per Capita (ppp)

We investigate the relationship between each individual capital and economic growth by using Figs. 3.7, 3.8, 3.9, 3.10, 3.11, and 3.12. The graphs have four dimensions: the X-axis changes from graph to graph (NIC, human capital, market capital, process capital, and renewal capital), the Y-axis is a fixed dimension of GDP per capita (ppp) in US dollars (hereafter termed GDP), the color shade represents renewal capital with red denoting higher levels of renewal capital, and the bubble size denotes the population of a country. Figure 3.7 is the relationship between NIC and GDP for all 48 countries. Figures 3.8, 3.9, 3.10, 3.11, and 3.12 display the co-development of the intellectual capital–GDP relationship over the 6-year time frame for the five countries. Since financial capital is the transformed 1–10 score from GDP, there is no need to plot its relationship against itself. In the figures, 2005 is the starting point tagged with the name of the country, and the end point is 2010.

In particular, Fig. 3.7 is plotted to clearly show a full picture of the relationship between NIC and GDP for 48 countries in 2010. The strong positive correlation

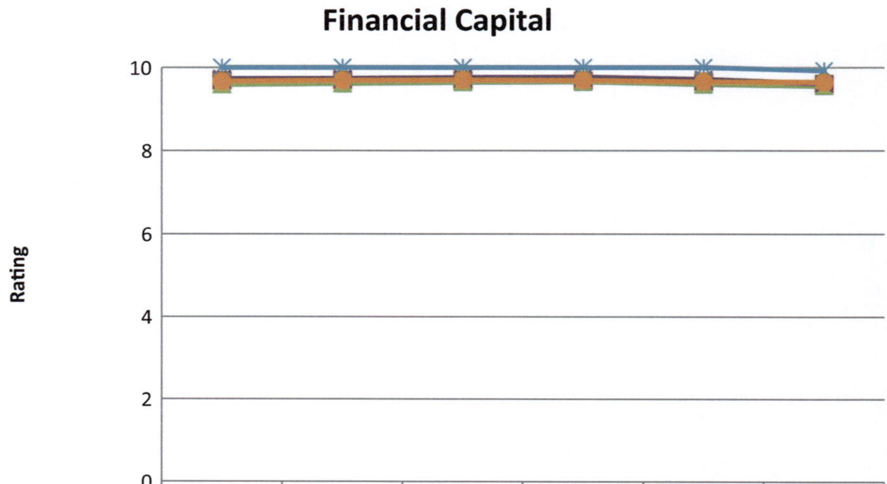

	2005	2006	2007	2008	2009	2010
Denmark	9.68	9.69	9.69	9.68	9.65	9.60
Finland	9.59	9.61	9.64	9.65	9.59	9.55
Iceland	9.72	9.73	9.75	9.76	9.71	9.60
Norway	10.00	10.00	10.00	10.00	10.00	9.92
Sweden	9.67	9.69	9.70	9.69	9.66	9.64

Fig. 3.5 Financial capital of Denmark, Finland, Iceland, Norway, and Sweden

indicates that the higher the NIC, the higher the GDP, and vice versa. Consequently, enhancing NIC is definitely a strategic issue that deserves the attention of national policy makers.

Figure 3.8 shows the formation of the NIC and GDP co-development continuum from the bottom left to the upper right. The paths of the five countries are located at the upper end of the continuum. The development of Denmark, Finland, and Sweden was intertwined with each other, with Finland joined the group starting in 2008. Iceland's path led farther and farther apart from these three countries over the years, due to its financial turmoil. The development indicates Iceland's large-scale NIC and modest scale GDP decline. Different from others, Norway's path was at the left side of the 48-country continuum tilted toward the GDP axis, indicating Norway had faster progress in GDP than in NIC. On the other hand, the paths of Denmark, Finland, and Sweden were tilted toward NIC axis, showing their faster NIC progress than GDP growth.

Figure 3.9 shows the co-development of human capital and GDP per capita (ppp) over the 6 years. The development pattern is somewhat similar to that of Fig. 3.8. We added a dotted arrow line to more clearly show the continuum of the 48 countries in year 2010. The path at the right side of the dotted line shows the progress of human capital is better than that of its GDP and vice versa for the path at the left

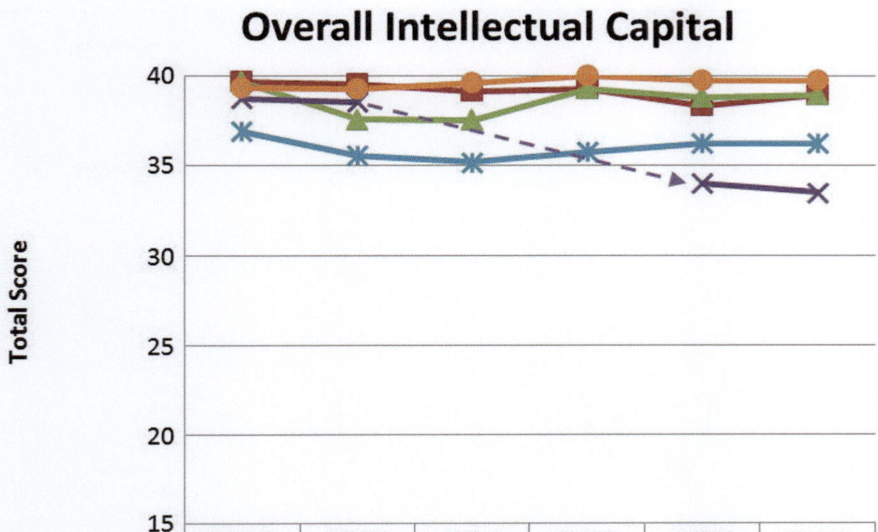

	2005	2006	2007	2008	2009	2010
Denmark	39.61	39.51	39.08	39.21	38.31	38.89
Finland	39.64	37.51	37.49	39.24	38.75	38.92
Iceland	38.71	38.48			33.96	33.47
Norway	36.86	35.52	35.16	35.74	36.18	36.23
Sweden	39.30	39.22	39.56	39.98	39.68	39.70

Fig. 3.6 NIC of Denmark, Finland, Iceland, Norway, and Sweden

side of the dotted line. Therefore, the development of human capital in Denmark, Finland, Iceland, and Sweden was better than that of their GDP on a 48-country landscape. Unlike Fig. 3.8, Finland's human capital and GDP co-development path was lower than that of Denmark, Iceland, and Sweden. Norway's development path was at the left side of the dotted line, meaning its GDP was better developed than its human capital. Several messages are apparent in Fig. 3.9. First, except Norway, these Nordic countries should consider enhancing the added value of human capital, as its development did not accompany with matching GDP growth as other countries in this dataset. Second, Iceland can utilize its human capital to revive the economy, as its human capital is in a relatively good position globally. Third, Finland has much higher student PISA performance than that of Denmark, Iceland, and Sweden; however, its human capital lagged behind these countries and deserves some attention. Fourth, although Norway is high on GDP growth, its relatively low human capital deserves special attention, as human capital is the very foundation of future intangible assets development.

Figure 3.10 shows the co-development of market capital and GDP per capita (ppp) with a spreading bubbles background rather than the continuum like the last

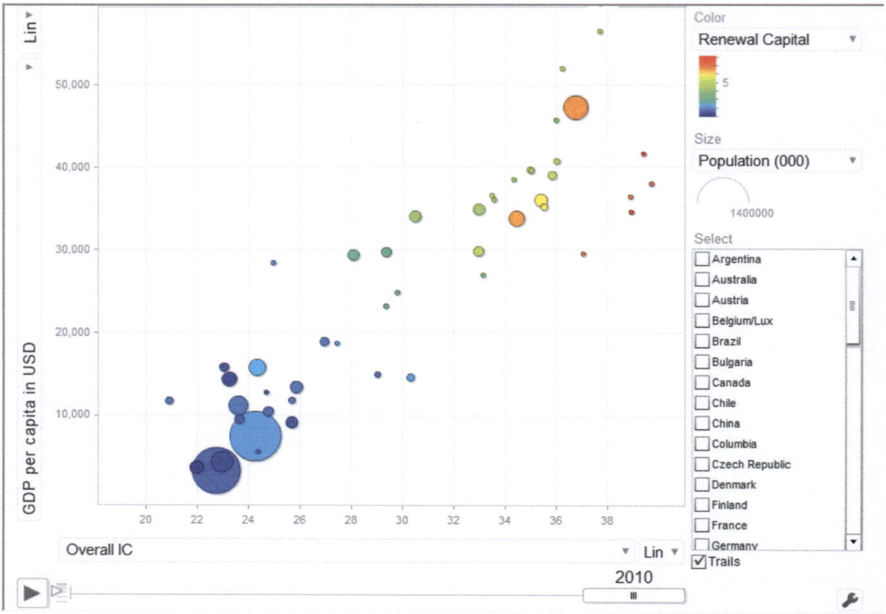

Fig. 3.7 NIC versus GDP per capita (ppp) for 48 countries in 2010

two figures. In other words, the correlation between market capital and GDP was not high for the 48 countries as a whole. It also shows that market capital of the Nordic countries was not necessarily better than that of developing countries. For example, market capital of Sweden in 2005 was only a little better than that of China and India (the two big bubbles at the bottom center of the graph), and the regressed market capital of Iceland in 2010 was much lower than that of China and India.

Again, the paths of Denmark, Finland, and Sweden were intertwined and at the higher end of the 48-country market capital landscape. Iceland's development pattern clearly went backward horizontally. That is, Iceland's market capital decline did not accompany with either increase or decrease of its GDP growth. In addition, its continuous decline started from 2006 has sent a warning before the outbreak of its financial system. Norway's vertical path tilted toward the GDP axis indicates that its GDP was better developed than its market capital.

Figure 3.11 shows the co-development of process capital and GDP per capita (ppp) over the 6 years. The 48 countries continuum appeared again. All process capital went backward, except Sweden. The paths of Denmark, Finland, and Sweden are at the upper right-hand side of the continuum, meaning their process capital developed better than their GDP growth. Iceland's process capital went backward first with some GDP growth then with a drop in GDP. Its path indicated that Iceland had a process capital decline earlier (from 2006) than its financial meltdown. Norway's path was still in the upper left-hand side of the continuum, yet

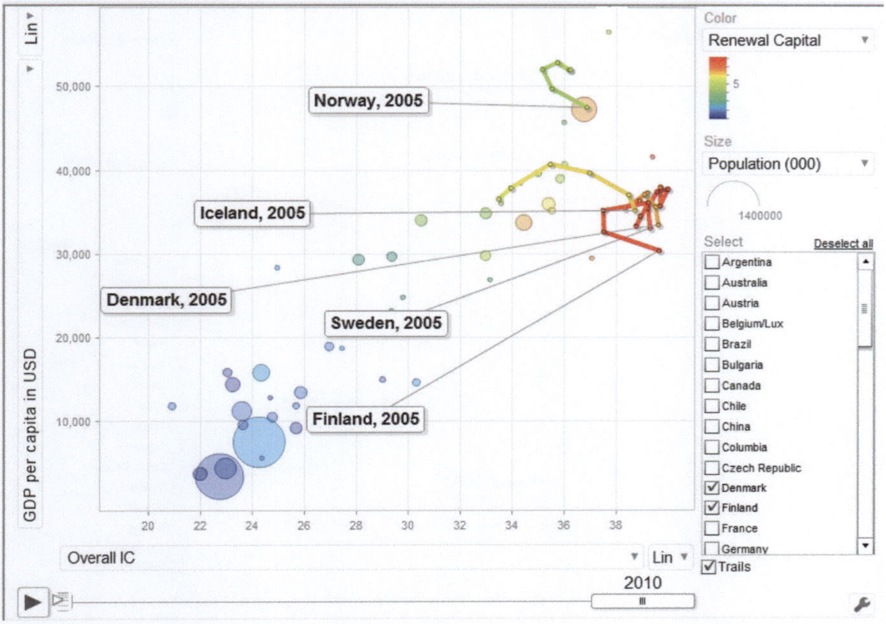

Fig. 3.8 The development of NIC and GDP per capita (ppp) for the Nordic countries from 2005 to 2010

it was much closer to that of the other countries in this graph. That is, Norway's process capital was at a similar level with other Nordic countries in 2005; however, it decreased over the years.

The message revealed in this figure is that the added value of process capital in the Nordic countries (except Norway) can be strengthened, as its progress did not accompany matching GDP growth, comparing to the 48-country norm.

Figure 3.12 shows the co-development of renewal capital and GDP per capita (ppp) over the 6 years. The 48-country continuum is still visible. Interestingly, the continuum moved more toward the GDP axis compared to previous figures. That is, in general, renewal capital co-developed with GDP growth better than NIC, human capital, and process capital. Again, the paths of all the countries (except Norway) are at the right-hand side of the dotted line. This phenomenon is more so for Finland and Sweden, meaning their renewal capital developed much better than their GDP growth. In addition, Iceland and Sweden had renewal capital decline during this period.

The meaning in this figure is that although renewal capital is higher in Finland and Sweden than the other countries, its added value needs to be greatly enhanced.

In summary, the above six figures uncover some distinctive development patterns. First, development paths of Denmark, Finland, and Sweden are generally clustered together, except for human capital and renewal capital. Second, renewal capital has more variation among these five countries. Third, most of the capitals of

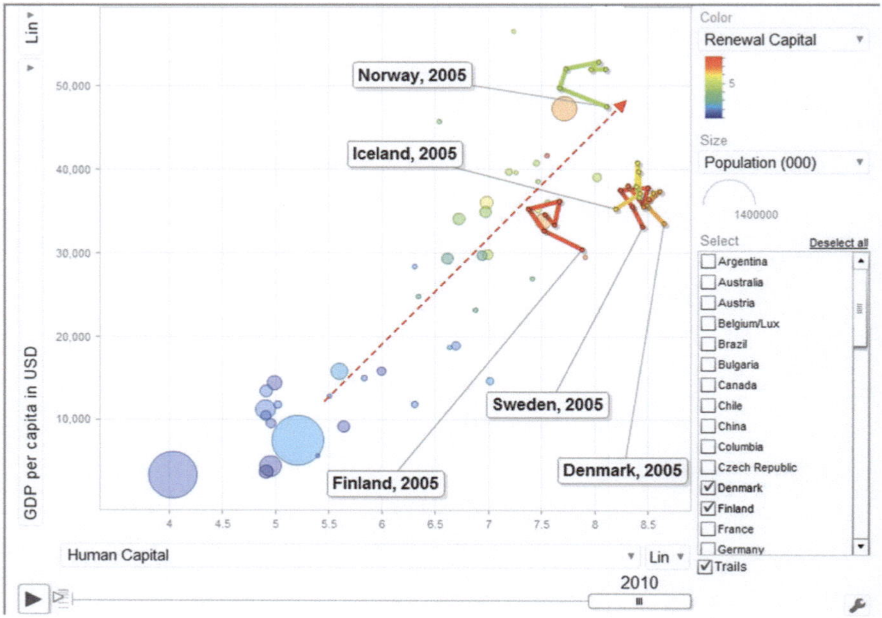

Fig. 3.9 The development of human capital and GDP per capita (ppp) for the Nordic countries from 2005 to 2010

Iceland dropped before its financial system breakdown. Fourth, the development path of Norway was generally separate from that of the other Nordic countries. Fifth, except Norway, the national intellectual capital of the other four countries developed much better than their GDP growth. Therefore, the added value of their intangible assets needs to be further enhanced.

Long-Term and Short-Term National Intellectual Capital

In addition to the above six figures that exhibit the relationship of each individual capital with GDP per capita (ppp), the following four figures further plot the relationships between human capital, market capital, process capital, and renewal capital. In our previous work (Lin & Edvinsson, 2011, p. 324), **we found that the combined increase in human capital and renewal capital will lead to a nation's long-term development**, whereas the combined increase in market capital and process capital may result in more immediate economic development. To present their relationships, Figs. 3.13, 3.14, 3.15, and 3.16 map the four capitals on a coordinate with two types of presentation. Based on the same data, Figs. 3.13 and 3.15 exhibit a scatterplot for the five countries only, whereas Figs. 3.14 and 3.16 show all 48 countries in the background so that readers will know the relative

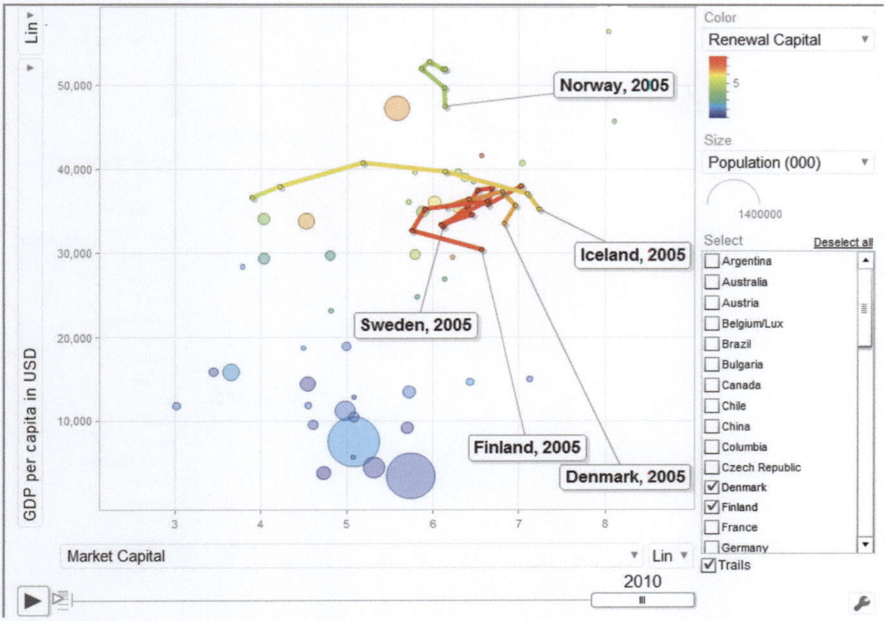

Fig. 3.10 The development of market capital and GDP per capita (ppp) for the Nordic countries from 2005 to 2010

positions of these five countries. Please note that the connotation of color shade for Figs. 3.14 and 3.16 has been changed from renewal capital to GDP per capita (ppp); that is, red represents high GDP per capita (ppp).

In terms of long-term NIC, both Figs. 3.13 and 3.14 indicate that Sweden was ahead of the other four countries in the upper right corner, meaning its human capital and renewal capital are both high. Yet, Swedish renewal capital dropped from 2008 onward; on the contrary, Denmark's renewal capital kept improving starting in 2007, even during the financial crisis. The renewal capital decrease in Sweden and increase in Denmark has led to the result that Denmark almost caught up with Sweden in 2010. This finding reflects the warning posed by researchers that during the last 20 years, the development of research with high international impact has been weaker in Sweden than in countries such as Denmark, the Netherlands, and Switzerland (Oquist & Benner, 2012; Stjernlöf, 2013). Norway was in the lower left corner, indicating its human capital and renewal capital were both relatively low comparing to the other countries. Denmark had better human capital than renewal capital and Finland had better renewal capital than human capital. Overall, Fig. 3.14 shows that the long-term-oriented human capital and renewal capital of the five countries were mainly at the higher end of the continuum.

Figures 3.15 and 3.16 map market capital and process capital of the five countries on a coordinate plane. Market capital refers to the general assets embodied in a nation's relationship with international markets, while process capital refers

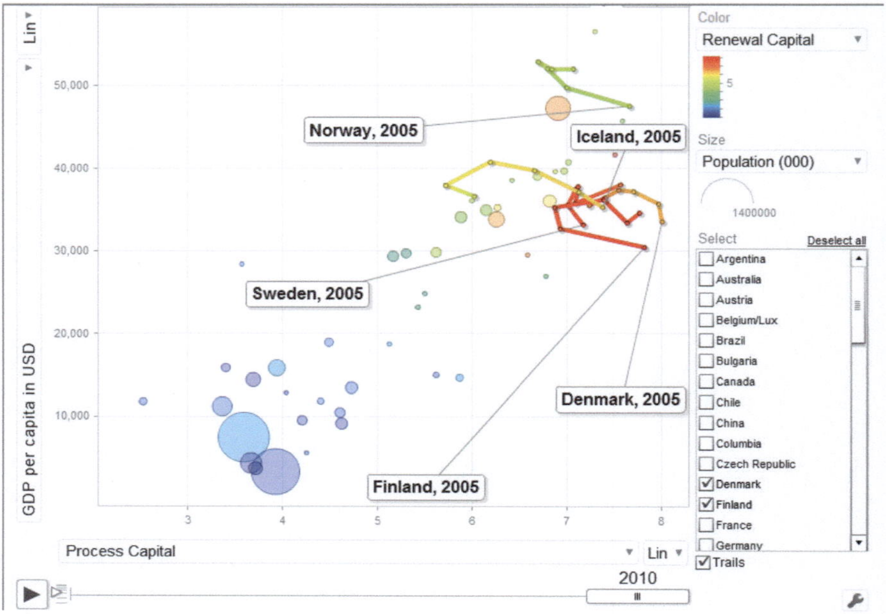

Fig. 3.11 The development of process capital and GDP per capita (ppp) for the Nordic countries from 2005 to 2010

to national infrastructure, such as information systems and the number of days required to start a new business. For short-term competition, these are two types of capital that can be expected to produce faster results if a nation is willing to engage in more extensive investments.

These two short-term NIC graphs indicate that the five Nordic countries are not too far apart from each other, except that Iceland dropped to the bottom left corner during the last 2 years (2009–2010). Figure 3.15 shows a warning sign for Denmark. Its position in the upper right corner in 2005 dropped more drastically from 2006 to 2009 than the other three countries (except Iceland). Although there was a rebound in 2010, its position was still lower than that of Finland and Sweden. Sweden had good short-term market capital and process capital progress from 2006 onward. Excluding Iceland, Norway had the lowest short-term market capital and process capital in this country cluster.

Overall, Fig. 3.16 shows that the short-term-oriented market capital and process capital of the Nordic countries were still at the higher end of the continuum, except for Iceland.

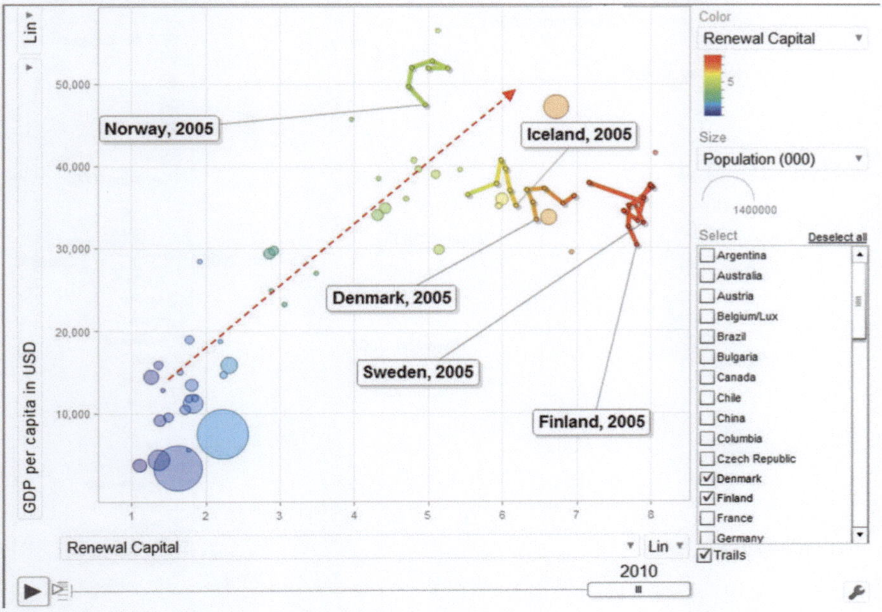

Fig. 3.12 The development of renewal capital and GDP per capita (ppp) for the Nordic countries from 2005 to 2010

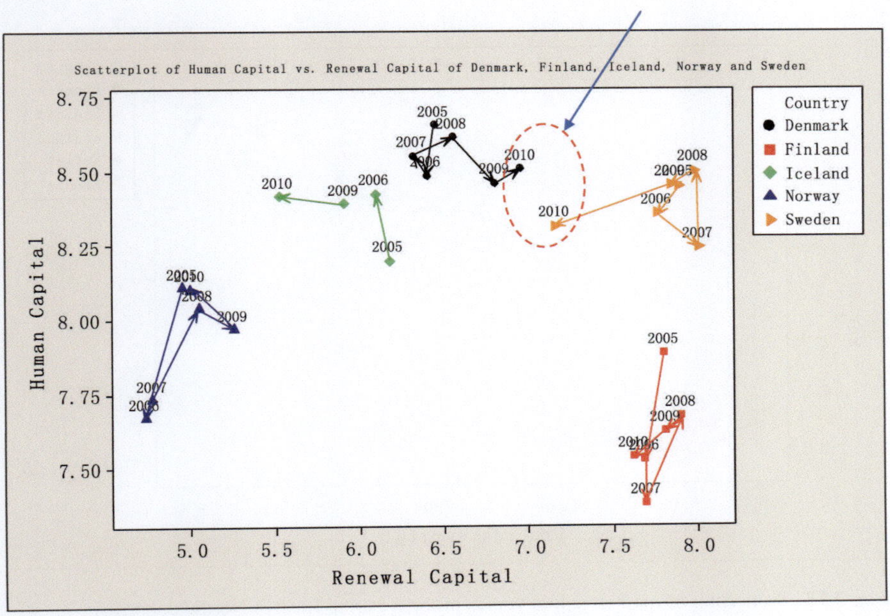

Fig. 3.13 Scatterplot of human capital versus renewal capital for five Nordic countries

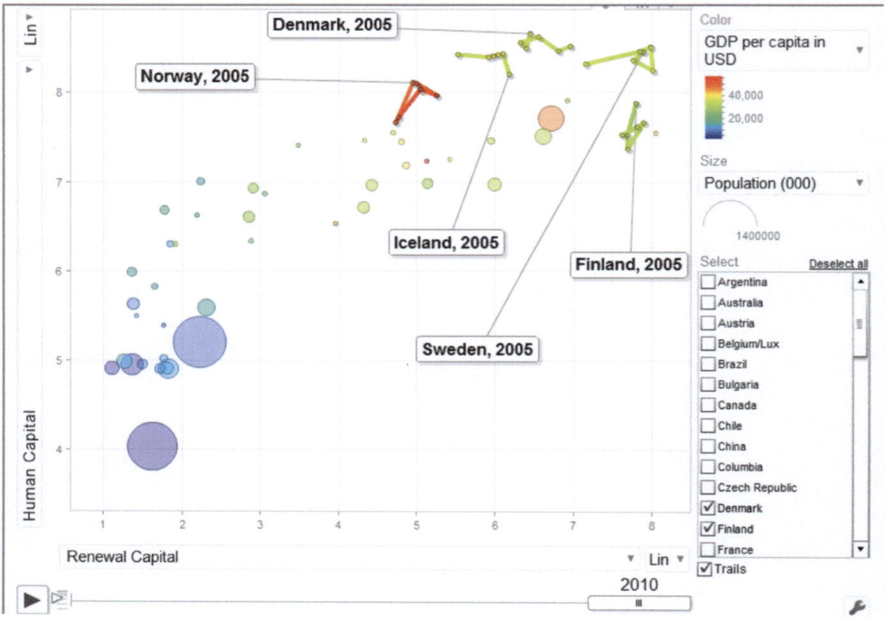

Fig. 3.14 Human capital versus renewal capital for five Nordic countries

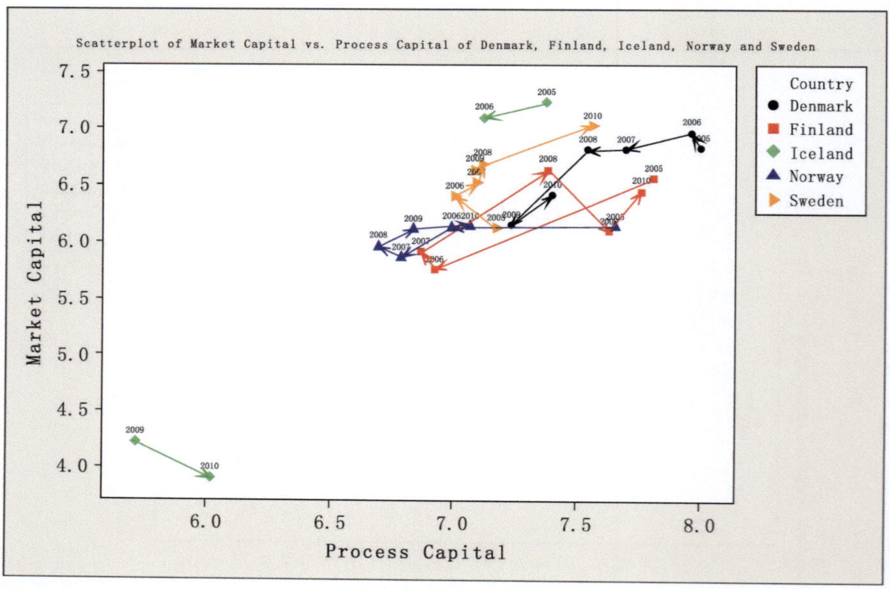

Fig. 3.15 Scatterplot of market capital versus process capital for five Nordic countries

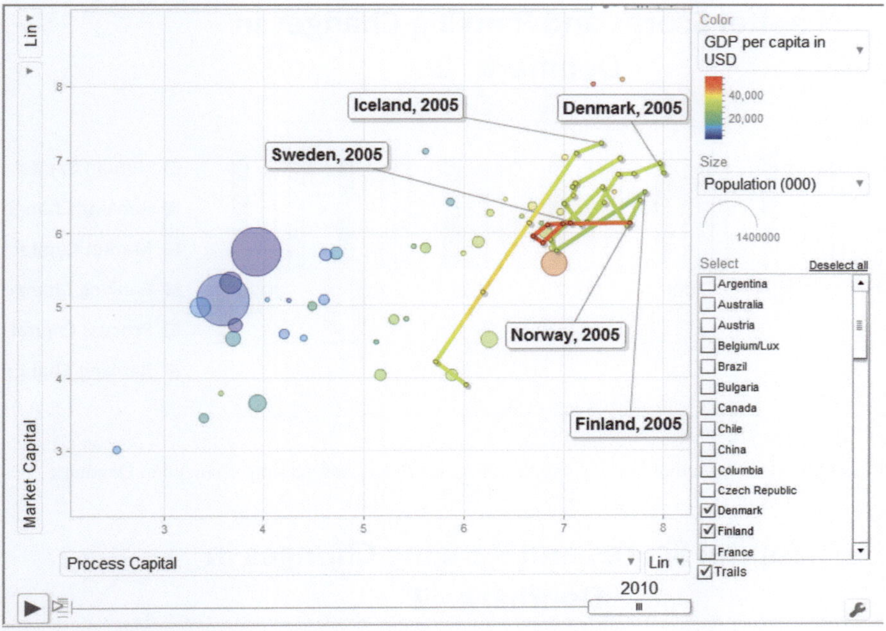

Fig. 3.16 Market capital versus process capital for five Nordic countries

Dynamics of National Intellectual Capital in Three Time Periods

The illustrations and graphs in the previous sections describe the internal progression of NIC in each country as individual capital scores change over the 6 years (Figs. 3.1, 3.2, 3.3, 3.4, 3.5, and 3.6) and the path of development of various capitals (Figs. 3.8, 3.9, 3.10, 3.11, and 3.12). The ranking changes that will be introduced in this section represent external competitiveness. Rankings, by and large, is a zero-sum game in which the advance of one country simultaneously marks the decline of another.

In order to probe the dynamics of NIC change before and after the financial crisis, we plotted Figs. 3.17, 3.18, 3.19, 3.20, 3.21, 3.22, 3.23, 3.24, 3.25, and 3.26 and Table 3.2 in three time periods: 2005–2006, 2007–2008, and 2009–2010. To have a clearer presentation, we separate the data in two sets. The first set contains capital scores and ranking changes of human capital, market capital, and process capital in Figs. 3.17, 3.19, 3.21, 3.23, and 3.25. The second set exhibits capital scores and ranking changes of renewal capital, financial capital, and average NIC in Figs. 3.18, 3.20, 3.22, 3.24, and 3.26.

The figures are mapped based on the mean capital scores and ranking changes of each period. Ranking changes in Figs. 3.17 to 3.26 are next to each capital score and copied from the bold-faced ranking difference of columns 2, 5, 7, and 9 of Table 3.2.

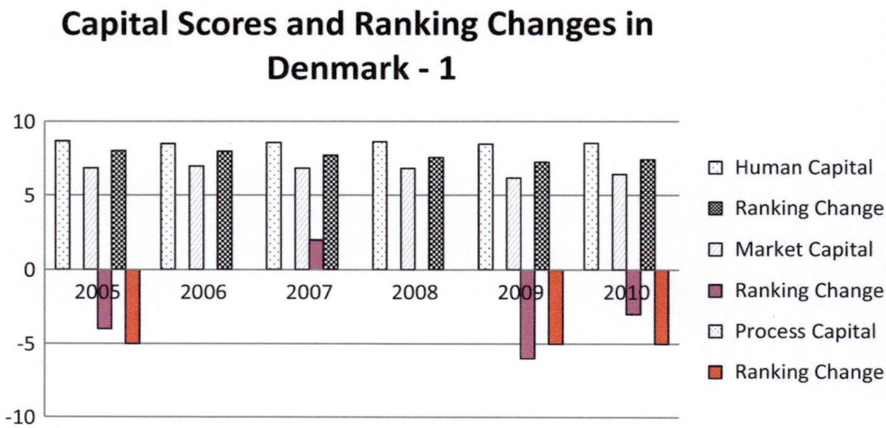

Fig. 3.17 Human capital, market capital, process capital, and ranking changes in Denmark

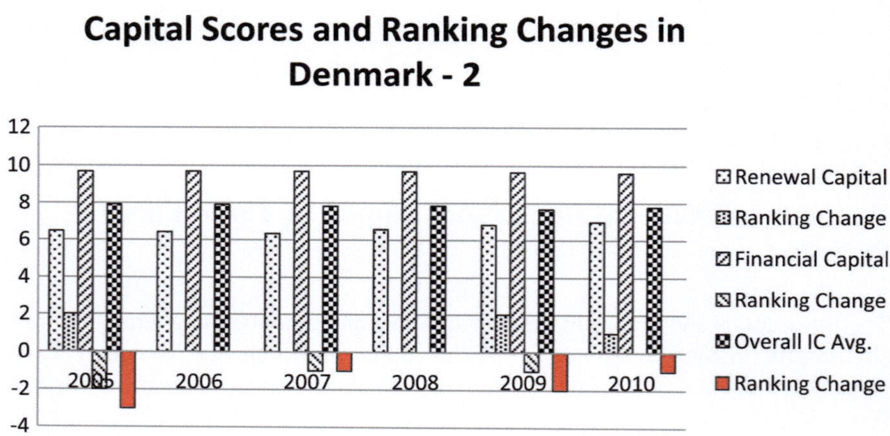

Fig. 3.18 Renewal capital, financial capital, average NIC, and ranking changes in Denmark

Taking market capital ranking difference of Denmark (−4, 2, −6, −3), for example, the ranking change of "−4," representing the difference between the third (2009–2010) and first (2005–2006) period, was plotted at 2005; the ranking change of "2," representing the difference between the second period (2007–2008) and first (2005–2006), was plotted at 2007; the ranking change of "−6," representing the difference between the third period (2009–2010) and second (2007–2008), was plotted at 2009; and the ranking change of "−3," representing the difference between the third period (2009–2010) and 6-year average ranking (exhibited in Table 3.1), was plotted at 2010. Special attention can be paid to the negative numbers, which indicate that the level of a particular capital was higher before

Fig. 3.19 Human capital, market capital, process capital, and ranking changes in Finland

Fig. 3.20 Renewal capital, financial capital, average NIC, and ranking changes in Finland

than after the financial crisis. Since it is easier to read figures than tables, we will describe the findings of each figure separately.

As shown in Fig. 3.17 and Table 3.2, Denmark (0, 0, 0, 0) did not have any human capital ranking change over the three time periods. However, it did experience relative large-scale negative ranking changes in market capital (−4, 2, −6, −3) and process capital (−5, 0, −5, −5). The last digit of −3 and −5 particularly indicated that Denmark lost international competitiveness in market capital and process capital in the most recent period (2009–2010), compared with its 6-year average ranking. Even though Figs. 3.2 and 3.3 show that its market capital score only decreased from 6.83 (2005) to 6.42 (2010) and process capital score decreased

Fig. 3.21 Human capital, market capital, process capital, and ranking changes in Iceland

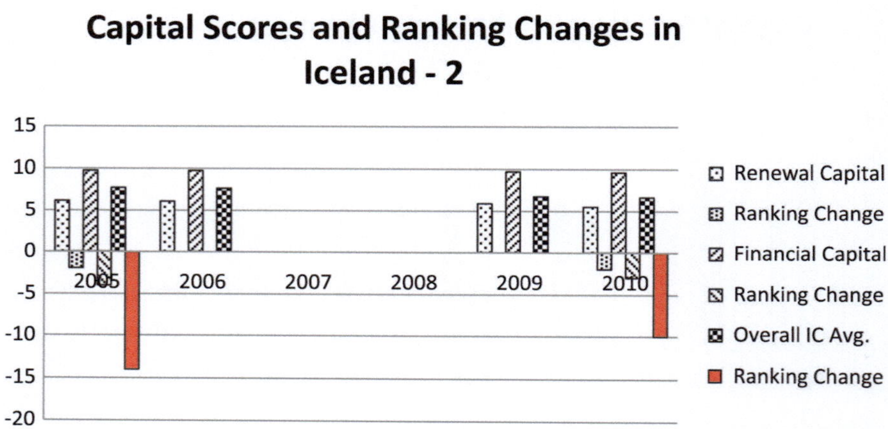

Fig. 3.22 Renewal capital, financial capital, average NIC, and ranking changes in Iceland

from 8.00 (2005) to 7.40 (2010), the ranking drop was large. This means, small internal variation may lose international competitiveness with a scale. Therefore, attending to both NIC internal improvement and external competitiveness at the same time is suggested.

Figure 3.18 shows that ranking changes of Denmark's renewal capital (2, 0, 2, 1), financial capital (−2, −1, −1, 0), and NIC (−3, −1, −2, −1) were relatively minor, especially the last digit change ranges from −1 to 1 only. However, the all positive ranking changes in renewal capital indicated that Denmark advanced its renewal capability over the years.

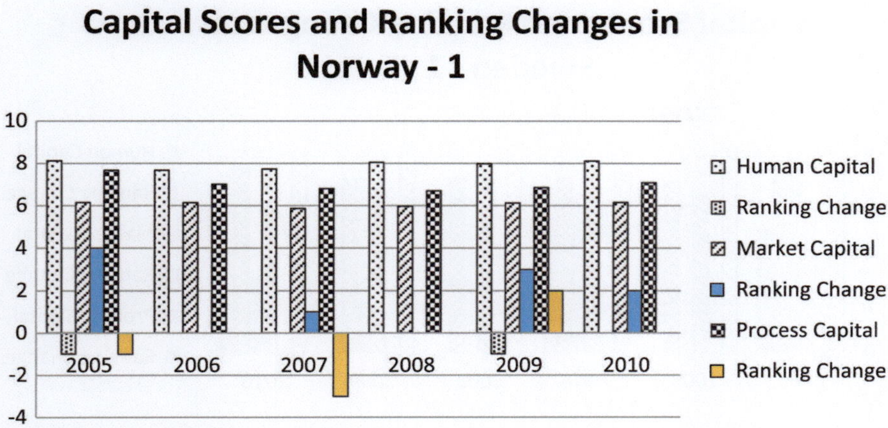

Fig. 3.23 Human capital, market capital, process capital, and ranking changes in Norway

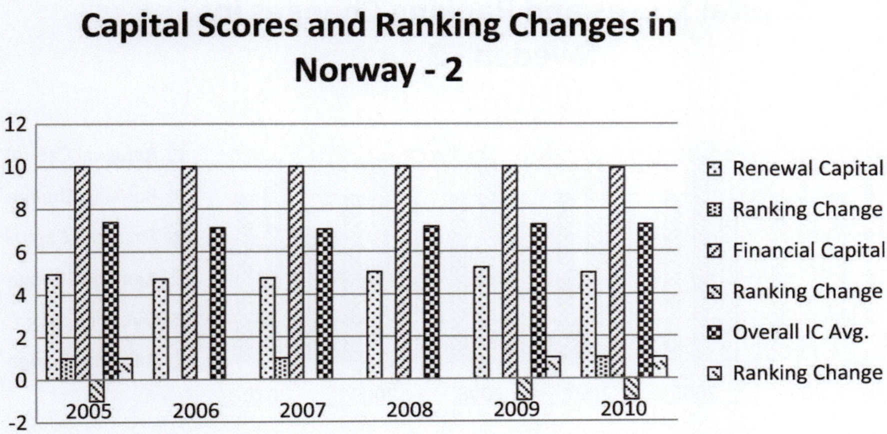

Fig. 3.24 Renewal capital, financial capital, average NIC, and ranking changes in Norway

As shown in Fig. 3.19 and Table 3.2, Finland did not have much human capital ranking changes (0, −1, 1, 0) over the three time periods. However, it did experience relative large-scale ranking gains in market capital (4, 5, −1, 0) and process capital (4, 1, 3, 2). Its negative market capital ranking change of −1 was minor, explained together with the last digit 0. The last positive digit of 2 particularly indicated that Finland gained international competitiveness in process capital in the most recent period (2009–2010), compared with its 6-year average ranking. In general, Finland gained international competitiveness in process capital after the financial crisis.

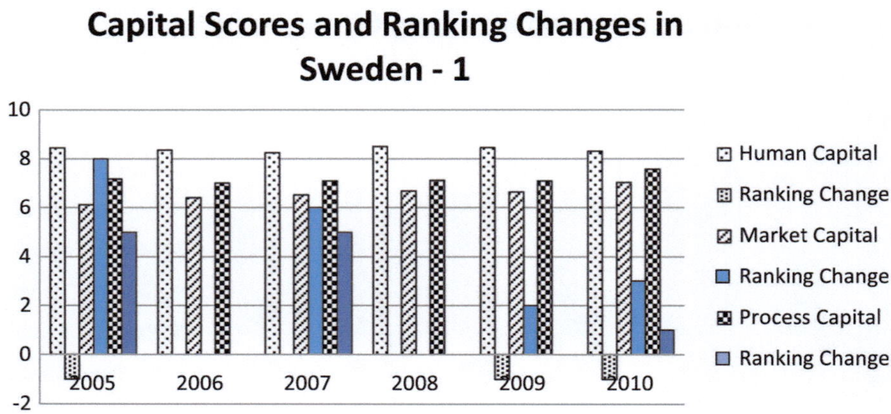

Fig. 3.25 Human capital, market capital, process capital, and ranking changes in Sweden

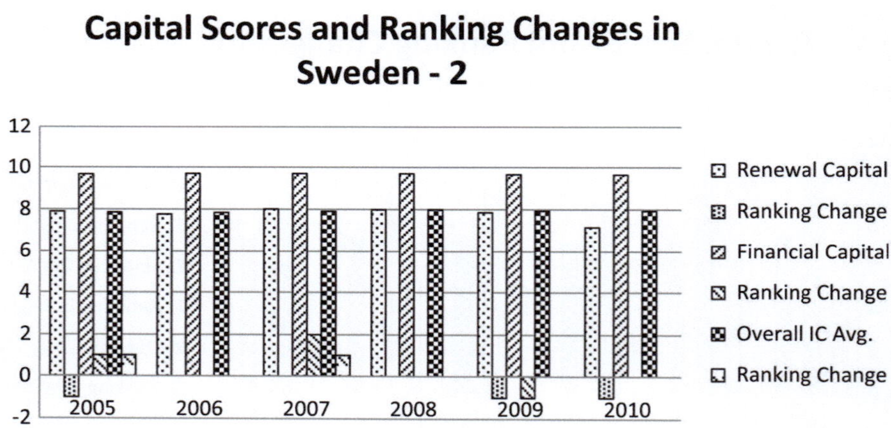

Fig. 3.26 Renewal capital, financial capital, average NIC, and ranking changes in Sweden

Figure 3.20 shows that ranking changes of Finland's renewal capital (1, 0, 1, 1), financial capital (0, 2, −2, 0), and NIC (2, 0, 2, 1) were minor. However, the two last digit of "1" indicated that Finland advanced its renewal capital and NIC after the financial crisis.

Iceland had incomplete data in this study, as our data source IMD did not provide data on Iceland for 2007 and 2008 due to its financial meltdown. From the available data in Fig. 3.21 and Table 3.2, Iceland did not have much human capital ranking changes (1, N/A, N/A, 1) over the three time periods. However, it did experience drastic ranking loss in market capital (−39, N/A, N/A, −22) and process capital (−15, N/A, N/A, −10). Its losing market capital international competitiveness in

Table 3.2 Ranking changes in three time periods for the five Nordic countries

	(First period–third period)	First period 2005–2006	Second period 2007–2008		Third period 2009–2010		Third period ranking versus overall NIC ranking	
Human capital	Difference#1	Ranking	Ranking	Difference	Ranking	Difference	NIC 48 ranking	Difference
Denmark	**0**	1	1	**0**	1	**0**	1	**0**
Finland	**0**	9	10	**−1**	9	**1**	9	**0**
Iceland	**1**	3	N/A	N/A	2	N/A	3	**1**
Norway	**−1**	4	4	**0**	5	**−1**	5	**0**
Sweden	**−1**	2	2	**0**	3	**−1**	2	**−1**
Market capital	Difference	Ranking	Ranking	Difference	Ranking	Difference	NIC 48 ranking	Difference
Denmark	**−4**	5	3	**2**	9	**−6**	6	**−3**
Finland	**4**	14	9	**5**	10	**−1**	10	**0**
Iceland	**−39**	4	N/A	N/A	43	N/A	21	**−22**
Norway	**4**	16	15	**1**	12	**3**	14	**2**
Sweden	**8**	12	6	**6**	4	**2**	7	**3**
Process capital	Difference	Ranking	Ranking	Difference	Ranking	Difference	NIC 48 ranking	Difference
Denmark	**−5**	1	1	**0**	6	**−5**	1	**−5**
Finland	**4**	5	4	**1**	1	**3**	3	**2**
Iceland	**−15**	7	N/A	N/A	22	N/A	12	**−10**
Norway	**−1**	6	9	**−3**	7	**2**	7	**0**
Sweden	**5**	10	5	**5**	5	**0**	6	**1**
Renewal capital	Difference	Ranking	Ranking	Difference	Ranking	Difference	NIC 48 ranking	Difference
Denmark	**2**	7	7	**0**	5	**2**	6	**1**
Finland	**1**	3	3	**0**	2	**1**	3	**1**
Iceland	**−2**	8	N/A	N/A	10	N/A	8	**−2**
Norway	**1**	15	14	**1**	14	**0**	15	**1**
Sweden	**−1**	2	2	**0**	3	**−1**	2	**−1**

(continued)

Table 3.2 (continued)

	(First period–third period)	First period 2005–2006	Second period 2007–2008		Third period 2009–2010		Third period ranking versus overall NIC ranking	
Financial capital	Difference	Ranking	Ranking	Difference	Ranking	Difference	NIC 48 ranking	Difference
Denmark	**−2**	11	12	**−1**	13	**−1**	13	**0**
Finland	**0**	17	15	**2**	17	**−2**	17	**0**
Iceland	**−4**	7	N/A	N/A	11	N/A	8	**−3**
Norway	**−1**	1	1	**0**	2	**−1**	1	**−1**
Sweden	**1**	13	11	**2**	12	**−1**	12	**0**
NIC	Difference	Ranking	Ranking	Difference	Ranking	Difference	NIC 48 ranking	Difference
Denmark	**−3**	1	2	**−1**	4	**−2**	3	**−1**
Finland	**2**	5	5	**0**	3	**2**	4	**1**
Iceland	**−14**	4	N/A	N/A	18	N/A	8	**−10**
Norway	**1**	9	9	**0**	8	**1**	9	**1**
Sweden	**1**	2	1	**1**	1	**0**	1	**0**

#Remarks

1. The second column compares the third (2009–2010) period ranking with the first (2005–2006)
2. The fifth column compares the second (2007–2008) period ranking with the first (2005–2006)
3. The seventh column compares the third (2009–2010) period ranking with the second (2007–2008)
4. The last column compares the most current third period ranking (2009–2010) with the original 6-year average NIC48 ranking summarized in Table 3.1

such a huge scale was particularly unexpected. This result is in concert with our finding that market capital and process capital are short-term NIC with faster consequences. Such devastating effect of ineffective national governance provided a good warning for future prevention.

Figure 3.22 shows the ranking changes of Iceland's renewal capital (−2, N/A, N/A, −1), financial capital (−4, N/A, N/A, −3), and NIC (−14, N/A, N/A, −10). Although not as large scale as market capital, Iceland's ranking decrease in NIC also deserve special attention when national intangibles become more and more important in national well-being.

As shown in Fig. 3.23 and Table 3.2, Norway did not have much human capital ranking changes (−1, 0, −1, 0) over the three time periods. However, it did experience relative large-scale ranking gains in market capital (4, 1, 3, 2), and both ranking loss and gain in process capital (−1, −3, 2, 0). Its last digit of "2" indicates that Norway gained international competitiveness in market capital in the most recent period (2009–2010) when compared with its 6-year average ranking. The two last digits of "0" representing its human capital and process capital in the most recent period remained the same as the 6-year average rankings.

Figure 3.24 shows that ranking changes for Norway's renewal capital (1, 1, 0, 1), financial capital (−1, 0, −1, −1), and NIC (1, 0, 1, 1) were minor. However, the last digit "1" of renewal capital and NIC indicate that Norway advanced these two areas after the financial crisis.

As shown in Fig. 3.25 and Table 3.2, Sweden did not have much of a change in human capital (−1, 0, −1, −1) over the three time periods. However, it did experience large-scale ranking gains in market capital (8, 6, 2, 3) and process capital (5, 5, 0, 1). Sweden was the only country in this cluster that had all positive ranking changes in these two short-term NIC. In other words, Sweden gained international competitiveness in market capital and process capital, even during and after the financial crisis.

Figure 3.26 shows that ranking changes of Sweden's renewal capital (−1, 0, −1, −1), financial capital (1, 2, −1, 0), and NIC (1, 1, 0, 0) were minor. However, its small-scale renewal capital decline after the financial crisis sends a signal for attention, as Sweden used to be very strong in renewal capital. This finding implies that other countries are catching up with Sweden in R&D and innovation.

In summary, for human capital ranking, the five Nordic countries had ranking gains as well as ranking losses at a relatively small scale. Market capital had the most drastic change, mainly due to Iceland's financial system breakdown. In general, Denmark lost international competitiveness in market capital after the financial crisis. On the contrary, Finland, Norway, and Sweden gained international competitiveness in market capital after the financial crisis with relatively large-scale ranking gains. For process capital, again Iceland had drastic ranking decline. Denmark also lost international competitiveness in process capital after the financial crisis. Yet, Finland and Sweden made gains in process capital.

For renewal capital, the ranking changes of the five countries are relatively small. Denmark, Finland, and Norway had all ranking gains, whereas Iceland and Sweden had ranking losses. For the 1–10 scale financial capital, the ranking variation of this country cluster was relatively small with some ups and downs. For NIC, again Iceland had a relatively large-scale ranking loss. Denmark had all ranking losses in all different period comparisons, whereas Finland, Norway, and Sweden had positive ranking changes, although the scale was relatively small.

Three-Dimensional National Intellectual Capital Trajectory

Up until this section, all the figures plotted different combinations of various types of capital, capital–GDP co-development, and ranking changes on a two-dimensional plane. Even though Figs. 3.7 to 3.12 displayed four dimensions with color and bubble size as the third and fourth dimension in addition to X-axis and Y-axis, graphically they are still on one plane. This section presents three-dimensional (3D) graphs showing each country's NIC development trajectory on a 48-country 3D landscape of various types. Since NIC evolution over time is always complex, combining different views from different angles may provide more comprehensive perspectives for analysis.

In what follows, we first explore the value-driving context by uncovering influencing factors of GDP growth for Denmark, Finland, Iceland, Norway, and Sweden from 2005 to 2010. Second, in explaining the GDP growth, we present the high, middle, and low capabilities which human capital, market capital, process capital, and renewal capital respectively have. Third, we examine the efficiency (GDP growth) enhancing and impeding factors of each country, taking each country's turning point into consideration. Last, we identify the efficiency drivers of each economy in reaching a targeted GDP.

Figure 3.27 shows a rectangular 3D landscape, with a longer north–south side. The formation of the landscape is based on the data of 29 national intellectual capital indicators (presented in Appendix 3) for 48 countries covering 6 years (2005–2010), with a total of 8,352 ($29 \times 48 \times 6$) data points. In other words, Fig. 3.27 is the aggregated NIC landscape of the 48 countries. The enlarged trails in Fig. 3.27 indicate NIC progression (upward), regression (downward), or configuration change (sideward) of each country over the 6-year period. Each white trail on the landscape represents a country. The altitude coloring from purple, dark blue, blue, green, yellow, to red is computer generated, according to GDP values, with purple representing high GDP and red low GDP. Figure 3.28 presents the potential rotation or partial presentation of the 3D formation in order to provide readers a better view for the focal area of discussion.

The relative NIC positions of Denmark, Finland, Iceland, Norway, and Sweden (pointed out with arrows) are mainly located at the upper left side of the overall landscape.

The following three figures – Figs. 3.29, 3.30, and 3.31 – form a set together. The areas of focus are shaded in light blue. Automated by the computer program to have a better view, the three figures are taken from left side view as Fig. 3.28 indicates. Figure 3.29 presents four graphs indicating the high capability region of human

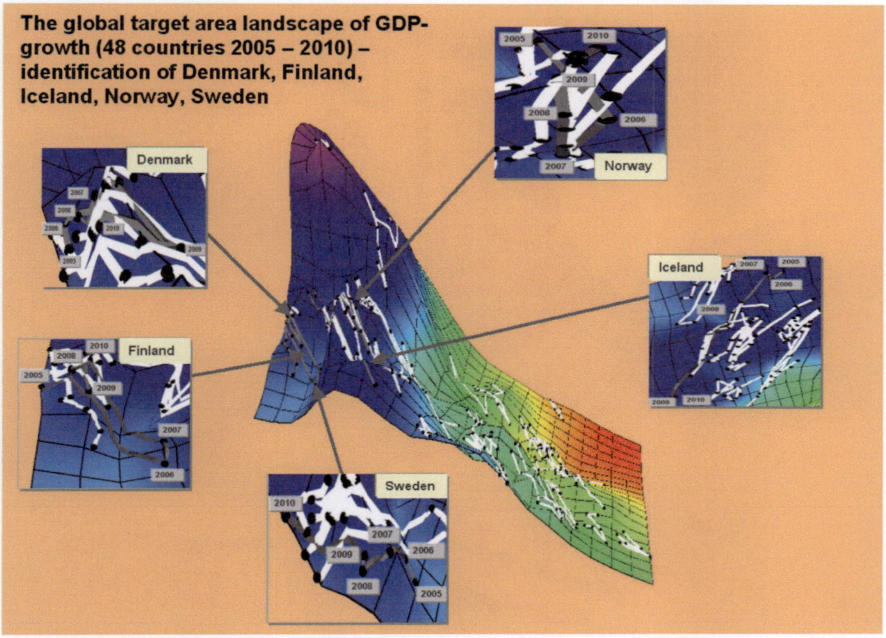

Fig. 3.27 The NIC trail of Denmark, Finland, Iceland, Norway, and Sweden on a 3D 48-country landscape

capital, market capital, process capital, and renewal capital in explaining the GDP growth. High capability means the data points are 20 % above the mean value of each capital. This figure shows that all the countries have all four capitals in the high capability region, except Iceland's market capital and process capital.

Figure 3.30 displays another four graphs indicating the middle capability region of each human capital, market capital, process capital, and renewal capital in explaining the GDP growth. Middle capability means the data points are within the top 50 % value of each capital. This figure shows that Iceland's market capital and process capital are in the middle capability region.

Figure 3.31 presents the last four graphs in this set and indicates the low capability region of each human capital, market capital, process capital, and renewal capital in explaining the GDP growth. Low capability means the data points are 20 % below the mean value of each capital. None of the capital of these five countries is in the low capability region.

In general, Figs. 3.29, 3.30, and 3.31 as a set explain that 90 % of the capitals (18 out of $4 \times 5 = 20$) of these five countries are in the high capability region in explaining GDP growth. In other words, these five Nordic countries are very competitive in national intangible assets among the 48 countries. In an era when intangible assets play an increasingly important role in national development, these Nordic countries are in a relatively advantageous position.

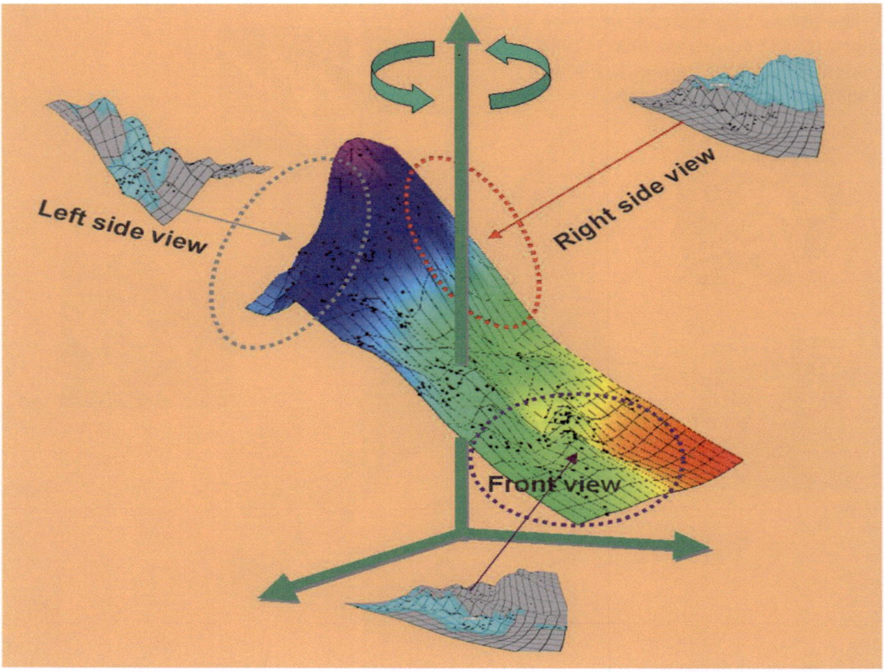

Fig. 3.28 The potential rotation and partial presentation of the 3D formation

Another set of figures, Figs. 3.32, 3.33, 3.34, 3.35, and 3.36 display efficiency enhancing or impeding factors that affect GDP growth before and after the NIC turning point for Denmark, Finland, Iceland, Norway, and Sweden, respectively. The white indicator boxes at the upper right display the results of the enhancing or impeding factors. All the five countries had one NIC turning point; therefore, we employed three rounds of data analysis. For instance, Denmark's turning point was 2009; therefore, we traced the explaining factors of 2005 against 2009 (starting point → the turning point), 2008 against 2009 (1 year before the turning point → the turning point), and 2009 against 2010 (the turning point → the ending point).

For an easy reference, we summarize in Table 3.3 two sets of results, each with the five key factors. If there is a clear percentage difference cutting point (such as less than 1 % in the white indicator boxes), the reported factors may be less than five. Results for the first set show the efficiency enhancing and impeding factors before the turning point. Results for the second set show the efficiency enhancing and impeding indicators after the turning point in italic letters. Since the factor strength (percentage) varies with different explaining power, we have calculated the average weight of the five enhancing and impeding factors and display each respective percentage in the rows for "Factor #5." We also count the frequency of four more frequently displayed categories, namely, government-related issues (G), human capital-related issues (H), market capital-related issues (M), and research

Fig. 3.29 The high capability region of human capital, market capital, process capital, and renewal capital

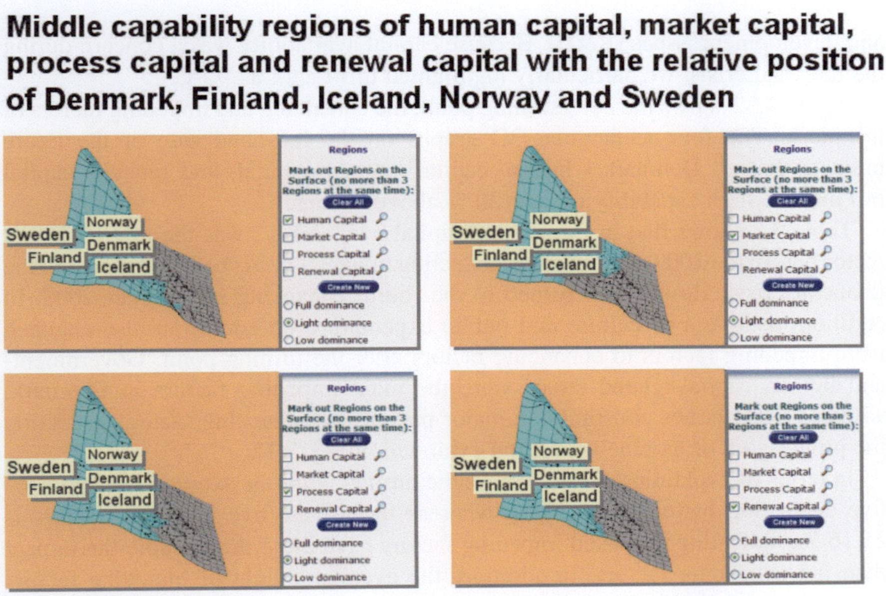

Fig. 3.30 The middle capability region of human capital, market capital, process capital, and renewal capital

Fig. 3.31 The low capability region of human capital, market capital, process capital, and renewal capital

and development issues (R&D). Because capital availability was a concern during the financial crisis, we particularly highlighted this factor as "G-C."

Figure 3.32 shows the 2009 turning point, the enhancing and impeding factors of Denmark. The four rectangular 3D graphs on the left-hand side of the figure indicate that all Denmark's human capital, process capital, and renewal capital fall into the high capability region (20 % above average).

Table 3.3 shows that in Denmark, "capital availability" was the first impeding factor before the 2009 turning point, reflecting financial needs before and during the financial crisis. However, it turned to the fourth enhancing factor after 2009. In addition, openness of culture and public expenditure on education also changed from impeding factors to enhancing factors after the turning point. Government- and human capital-related issues were the main impeding factors in Denmark, whereas R&D issues constituted a major part of the enhancing factors, reflecting the progression of its renewal capital exhibited in Fig. 3.12.

In terms of explaining power, before the turning point the average weight of the five enhancing factors is 11.32 %, whereas that of the five impeding factors is 25.16 %, indicating the listed impeding factors have more than double the impact than the enhancing factors. In addition, the average weight of impeding factors before the turning point (25.16 %) is more than doubled the weight after the turning point (11.61 %), reflecting Denmark's recovery after the financial crisis.

Figure 3.33 shows the 2007 turning point, the enhancing and impeding factors for Finland. The four rectangular 3D graphs on the left-hand side of the figure

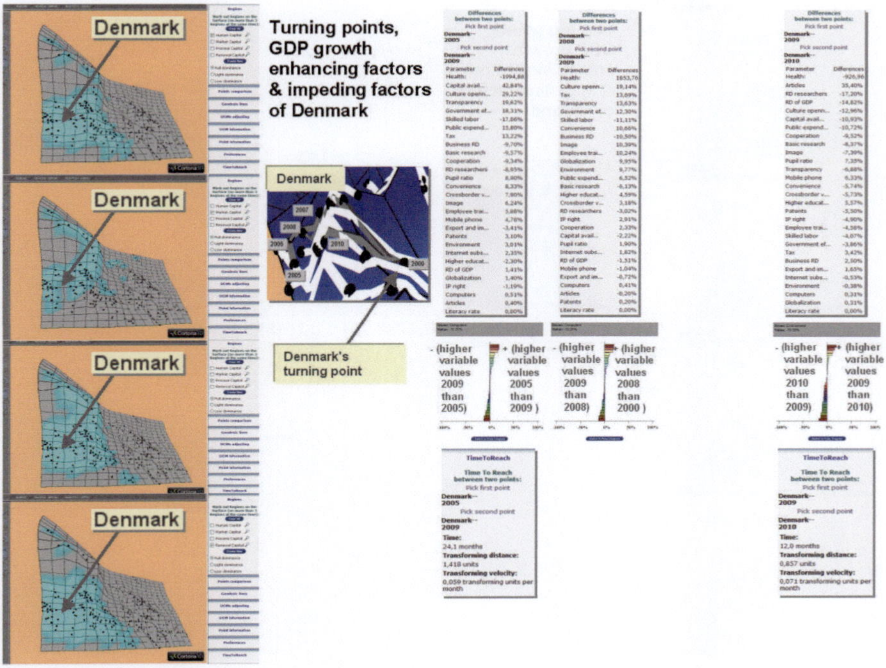

Fig. 3.32 Turning point and GDP growth enhancing and impeding factors of Denmark

indicate that Finland's human capital, process capital, and renewal capital fall into the high capability region (20 % above average).

Table 3.3 shows that in Finland, the first impeding factor "capital availability" before the 2007 turning point was turned into the second enhancing factor after the turning point. Another two impeding factors that turned positive after the turning point are skilled labor and transparency of government policy. On the contrary, the first enhancing factor "patents" before the 2007 turning point became the third impeding factor after the turning point. Government- and human capital-related issues are the main impeding factors in Finland. According to the relatively high average weight (27.46 %) of impeding factors before the turning point, employee training and government efficiency are the two factors that deserve special attention, excluding the three factors that turned to enhancing factors. However, the average weight (13.99 %) of impeding factors after the turning point has been greatly reduced comparing to that before the turning point, reflecting Finland's relatively sound situation during the financial crisis (after 2007). In addition to the abovementioned factors, convenience of establishing new firms and fair business competition environment are the two government-related enhancing factors that reflect the free business environment in Finland.

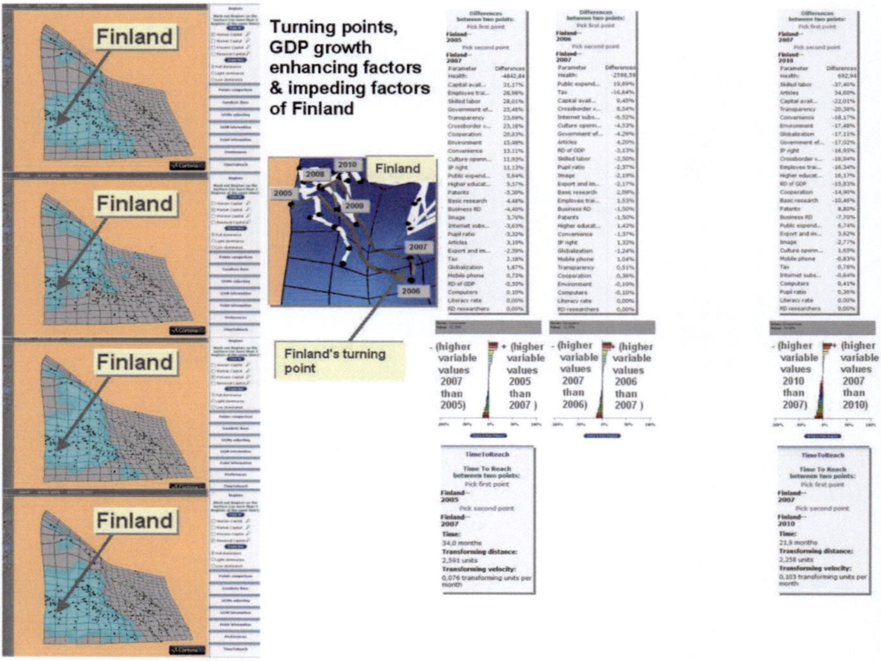

Fig. 3.33 Turning point and GDP growth enhancing and impeding factors of Finland

Figure 3.34 shows the 2007 turning point, the enhancing and impeding factors of Iceland. The four rectangular 3D graphs on the left-hand side of the figure indicate that Iceland's human capital and renewal capital fall into the high capability region (20 % above average). However, its market capital and process capital are in the middle capability region, mainly because of the relatively large-scale decline after its financial meltdown. The finding agrees with what mentioned earlier that these two capitals are short-term NIC, susceptible to external impact.

According to Table 3.3, Iceland's first impeding factor "capital availability" before the 2007 turning point has shown its financial trouble before the outburst of the 2008 global financial crisis. Its exceptionally high average weight (59.14 %) of impeding factors after the turning point truly reflects Iceland's troubles after 2007, especially in the areas of cross-border ventures, corporate tax encouragement, transparency of government policy, and image of country. Corporate tax encouragement changed from an enhancing factor to an impeding factor after 2007. However, skilled labor is an impeding factor, but became an enhancing factor after the turning point. For enhancing factors, human capital-related issues including employee training, pupil–teacher ratio, and public expenditure on education are the main drivers of its GDP growth.

Figure 3.35 shows the 2007 turning point, the enhancing and impeding factors of Norway. The four rectangular 3D graphs on the left-hand side of the figure indicate

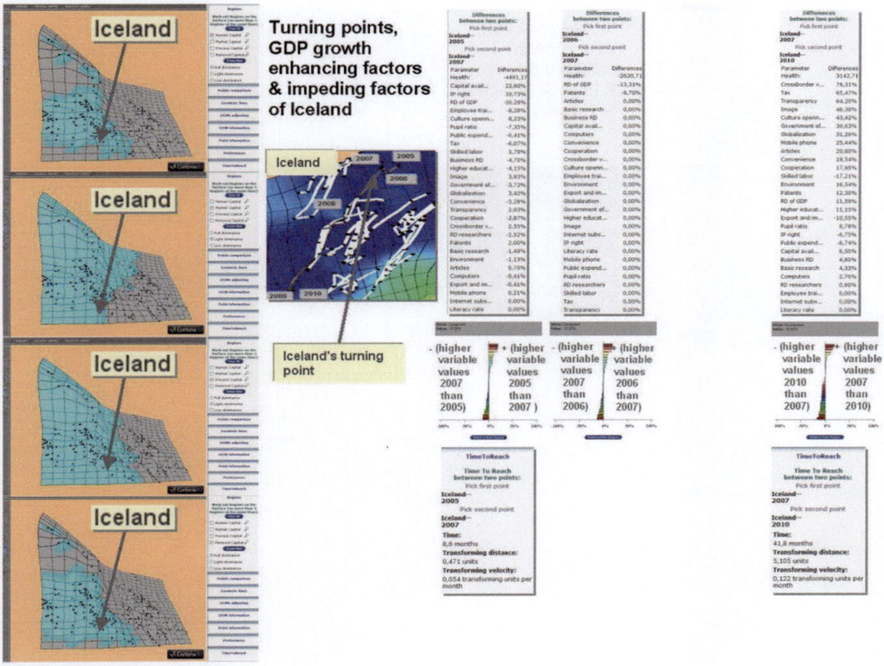

Fig. 3.34 Turning point and GDP growth enhancing and impeding factors of Iceland

that all Norway's human capital, process capital, and renewal capital fall into the high capability region (20 % above average).

Table 3.3 shows that in Norway, the first impeding factor "capital availability" before the 2007 turning point was turned into an enhancing factor after the turning point. Actually, Norway has the highest GDP per capita (ppp) in US dollars among the 48 countries. It has the largest pension fund in the world, which the country manages cautiously. During the financial crisis, Norway provided some funds for the IMF to assist countries in need (Halvorsen, 2009). There are three more impeding factors that were turned to enhancing factors after the turning point, including skilled labor, transparency of government policy, and university–enterprise cooperation. The reduced average weight of impeding factors after the turning point (12.87 % vs. 23.46 %) indicates Norway's relatively good status after 2007. For enhancing factors, although R&D issues constitute a major part, the influence was minor because of the small average weight of 4.05 % before the turning point. However, the average weight of 22.92 % after the turning point indicates increased influence of the enhancing factors, including university–enterprise cooperation and IP rights protection.

Figure 3.36 shows the 2008 turning point, the enhancing and impeding factors of Sweden. The four rectangular 3D graphs on the left-hand side of the figure indicate

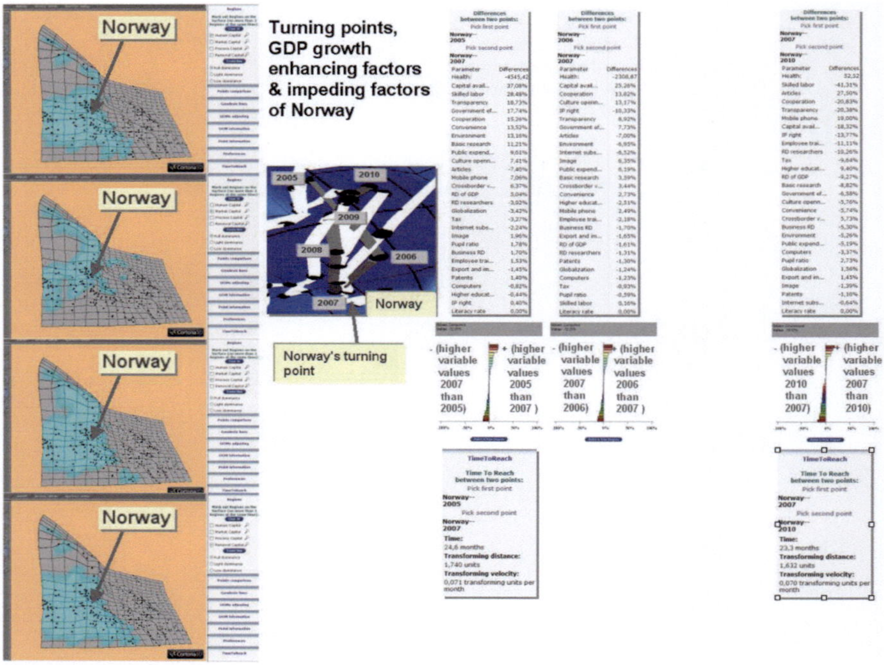

Fig. 3.35 Turning point and GDP growth enhancing and impeding factors of Norway

that all Sweden's human capital, market capital, process capital, and renewal capital fall into the high capability region (20 % above average).

According to Table 3.3, Sweden did experience some financial stress during the financial crisis, having "capital availability" as its second impeding factor. R&D issues accounted the most for its impeding factors, including scientific articles, business R&D, patents, and so on. This finding reflects Sweden's declining renewal capital, exhibited in Figs. 3.13 and 3.14. In addition, higher education enrollment was an impeding factor both before and after the turning point. Another human capital issue, public expenditure on education, was an impeding factor after the turning point. Since human capital and renewal capital are long-term-oriented NIC, the results send a warning signal that Sweden may lose its long-term NIC if coping measures are not taken. For enhancing factors, government-related issues are the major components, including transparency of government policy, government efficiency, fair business competition environment, and convenience of establishing new firms. Sweden did enjoy the efficiency of its government operation from how it weathered the financial crisis.

To summarize Table 3.3 into an overall suggestion, we count the frequency of both enhancing and impeding factors by categories for all the five countries, shown in the last row of the table. There are a total of 29 counts of government-related

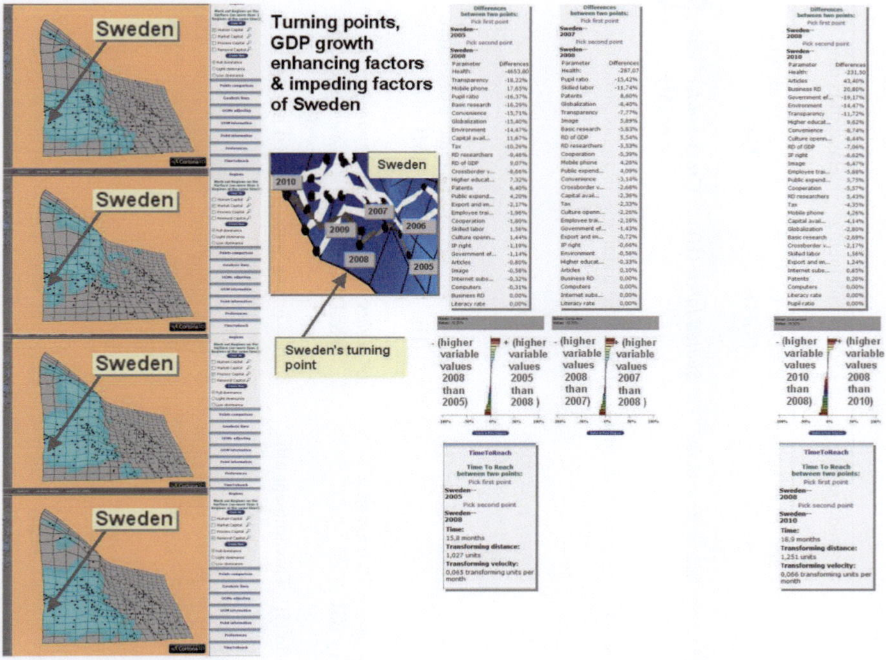

Fig. 3.36 Turning point and GDP growth enhancing and impeding factors of Sweden

issues (G). Among which 14 counts are impeding factors. Denmark and Finland have the largest count (4) of government-related issues as the impeding factors, followed by 3 counts of Iceland and Norway.

There are 25 counts of human capital issues (H). Among which 14 counts are impeding factors. Finland has the largest count (4) of human capital-related issues as the impeding factors, followed by 3 counts of Denmark, Norway, and Sweden. There are 14 counts of market capital issues (M), with 8 counts of impeding factors. Iceland had the largest count of 5. For research and development issues (R&D), there are 25 counts, among which impeding factors total 11 counts. Sweden has the largest count of 5.

Figure 3.37 identifies the efficiency drivers (positive term) for each individual country. Efficiency targeting is like benchmarking. Efficiency represents the GDP in this 3D software program. Since the Nordic countries are very advanced in terms of tangible and intangible assets, it is not easy to find a benchmark for these five countries. The rationale of choosing Switzerland as a benchmark is because it ranks number two in NIC (next to Sweden only) and number one in renewal capital. Although Switzerland's GDP per capita (ppp) is lower than that of Norway, it surpasses the other four countries. Therefore, Switzerland's GDP was chosen to be the efficiency target in Fig. 3.37. In this figure, the stacked small horizontal stripes are the deficiency factors of each economy benchmarked against Switzerland's

Table 3.3a Enhancing factors and impeding factors of GDP per capita (ppp) growth for the five Nordic countries

Influencing factor	Denmark enhancing factors	Denmark impeding factors	Finland enhancing factors	Finland impeding factors	Iceland enhancing factors	Iceland impeding factors
Factor #1 before (first) turning point	Skilled labor (H)	Capital availability (G-C)	Patents (R&D)	Capital availability (G-C)	R&D % GDP (R&D)	Capital availability (G-C)
Factor#1 after (last) turning point	*R&D researchers* (R&D)	*Scientific articles* (R&D)	*Skilled labor* (H)	*Scientific articles* (R&D)	*Skilled labor* (H)	*Cross-border ventures* (M)
Factor #2 before (first) turning point	Business R&D (R&D)	Openness of culture (M)	Basic research (R&D)	Employee training (H)	Employee training (H)	IP rights protection (R&D)
Factor #2 after (last) turning point	*R&D % GDP (R&D)*	*Pupil–teacher ratio* (H)	*Capital availability* (G-C)	*Higher education enrollment* (H)	*Export of goods* (M)	*Corporate tax encouragement* (G)
Factor #3 before (first) turning point	Basic research (R&D)	Transparency of government policy (G)	Internet subscribers	Skilled labor (H)	Pupil–teacher ratio (H)	Openness of culture (M)
Factor #3 after (last) turning point	*Openness of culture* (M)	*Mobile phone subscribers*	*Transparency of government policy* (G)	*Patents* (R&D)	*IP rights protection* (R&D)	*Transparency of government policy* (G)
Factor #4 before (first) turning point	R&D researchers (R&D)	Government efficiency (G)	Pupil–teacher ratio (H)	Government efficiency (G)	Public expenditure on education (H)	Skilled labor (H)
Factor #4 after (last) turning point	*Capital availability* (G-C)	*Higher education enrollment* (H)	*Convenience of establishing new firms* (G)	*Public expenditure on education* (H)	*Public expenditure on education* (H)	*Image of country* (M)
Factor #5 before (first) turning point	–	Public expenditure on education (H)	Export of goods (M)	Transparency of government policy (G)	Corporate tax encouragement (G)	Image of country (M)
	(Average weight – 11.32 %)	**(Average weight – 25.16 %)**	**(Average weight – 3.85 %)**	**(Average weight – 27.46 %)**	**(Average weight – 7.68 %)**	**(Average weight – 10.26 %)**

Factor #5 after (last) turning point	*Public expenditure on education* (H) **(Average weight – 13.33 %)**	*Corporate tax encouragement* (G) **(Average weight – 11.61 %)**	*Fair business competition environment* (G) **(Average weight – 23.09 %))**	*Export of goods* (M) **(Average weight– 13.99 %)**	– **(Average weight – 10.31 %)**	*Openness of culture* (M) **(Average weight – 59.14 %)**
Category frequency count	G – 1 H – 2 M – 1 R&D – 5	G – 4 H – 3 M – 1 R&D – 1	G – 4 H – 2 M – 1 R&D – 2	G – 4 H – 4 M – 1 R&D – 2	G – 1 H – 5 M – 1 R&D – 2	G – 3 H – 1 M – 5 R&D – 1

Table 3.3b Enhancing factors and impeding factors of GDP per capita (ppp) growth for the five Nordic countries

Influencing factor	Norway enhancing factors	Norway impeding factors	Sweden enhancing factors	Sweden impeding factors
Factor #1 before (first) turning point	Scientific articles (R&D)	Capital availability (G-C)	Transparency of government policy (G)	Mobile phone subscribers
Factor#1 after (last) turning point	*Skilled labor* (H)	*Scientific articles* (R&D)	*Government efficiency* (G)	*Scientific articles* (R&D)
Factor #2 before (first) turning point	R&D researchers (R&D)	Skilled labor (H)	Pupil–teacher ratio (H)	Capital availability (G-C)
Factor #2 after (last) turning point	*University–enterprise cooperation* (R&D)	*Mobile phone subscribers*	*Fair business competition environment* (G)	*Business R&D* (R&D)
Factor #3 before (first) turning point	Globalization (M)	Transparency of government policy (G)	Basic research (R&D)	R&D % GDP (R&D)
Factor #3 after (last) turning point	*Transparency of government policy* (G)	*Higher education enrollment* (H)	*Transparency of government policy* (G)	*Higher education enrollment* (H)
Factor #4 before (first) turning point	Corporate tax encouragement (G)	Government efficiency (G)	Convenience of establishing new firms (G)	Higher education enrollment (H)
Factor #4 after (last) turning point	*Capital availability* (G-C)	*Cross-border ventures* (M)	*Convenience of establishing new firms* (G)	*Public expenditure on education* (H)
Factor #5 before (first) turning point	Internet subscribers	University–enterprise cooperation (R&D)	Globalization (M)	Patents (R&D)
	(Average weight – 4.05 %)	**(Average weight– 23.46 %)**	**(Average weight – 16.40 %)**	**(Average weight – 10.42 %)**
Factor #5 after (last) turning point	*IP rights protection* (R&D)	*Pupil–teacher ratio* (H)	*Openness of culture* (M)	*R&D researchers* (R&D)
	(Average weight – 22.92 %)	**(Average weight – 12.87 %)**	**(Average weight – 12.51 %)**	**(Average weight – 17.00 %)**

Category frequency count	G – 3 H – 1 M – 1 R&D – 4	G – 3 H – 3 M – 1 R&D – 2	G – 6 H – 1 M – 2 R&D – 1	G – 1 H – 3 M – 0 R&D – 5
Category frequency count – **Grand total**	G –15 H – 11 M – 6 R&D – 14	G – 14 H – 14 M –8 R&D – 11		

Remarks: (G and G-C) – government-related issues including capital availability represented by G-C (total 29 counts including 8 counts of capital availability), (H) – human capital issues (25 counts), (M) – market capital issues (14 counts), (R&D) – research and development (25 counts)

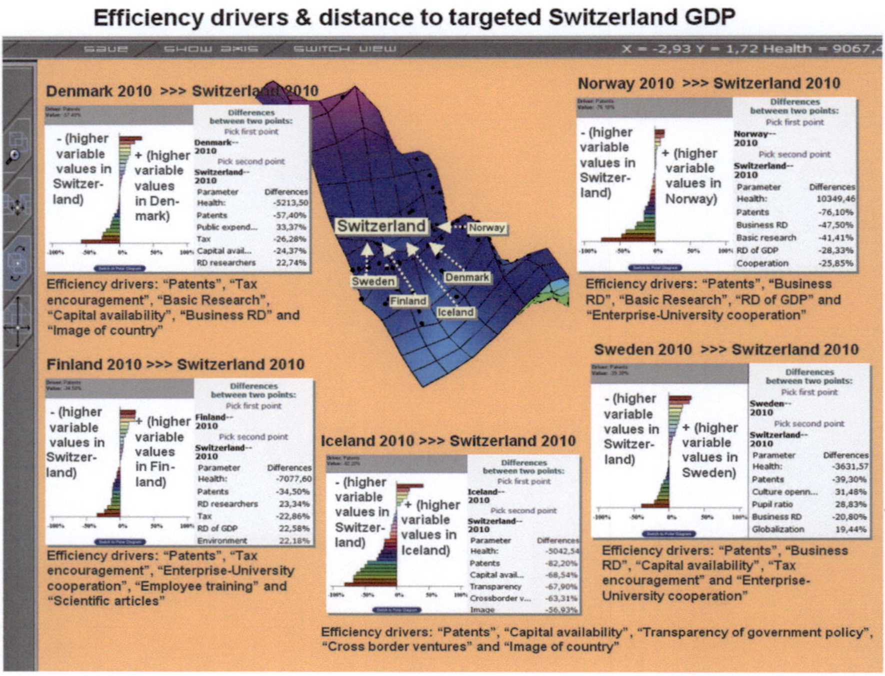

Fig. 3.37 Efficiency drivers and distance to targeted GDP of Switzerland

GDP in 2010. The length of the stripes represents the degree of deficiency. For easier comparison, we list the first five deficiency factors of each economy in Table 3.4.

With Switzerland being used as the benchmarking country, irrespective to the sequence of deficiency, the common areas (in frequency count) that these five countries need to improve include patents (5 counts), capital availability (3 counts), business R&D (3 counts), corporate tax encouragement (3 counts), university–enterprise cooperation (3 counts), basic research (2 counts), and image of country (2 counts). Although already advanced, these five Nordic countries need to improve "patents" the most when comparing to Switzerland. Out of the seven common factors, R&D issues cover four, government issues cover two, and the rest is market capital issue. Apparently, R&D is still the concern in order to catch up with Switzerland's growth.

Figure 3.37 shows that the efficiency distance of these five countries is not too far from Switzerland. Based on the average deficiency (negative term) percentage reported in Table 3.4, Iceland has the longest distance (−67.78 %) to achieve the targeted GDP of Switzerland, followed by Norway (−43.84 %), Denmark (−28.28 %), Sweden (−20.47 %), and Finland (−20.20 %).

The value of the above 3D trajectory analysis is to (1) display the NIC trails of the discussed countries on a 48-country landscape; (2) locate the capability region

Table 3.4 The first five efficiency drivers targeting GDP of Switzerland

Efficiency driver	Denmark	Finland	Iceland	Norway	Sweden
Factor #1	Patents	Patents	Patents	Patents	Patents
Factor #2	Corporate tax encouragement	Corporate tax encouragement	Capital availability	Business R&D	Business R&D
Factor #3	Capital availability	Basic research	Transparency of government policy	Basic research	Capital availability
Factor #4	Business R&D	University–enterprise cooperation	Cross-border ventures	R&D % GDP	Corporate tax encouragement
Factor #5	Image of country	Employee training	Image of country	University–enterprise cooperation	University–enterprise cooperation
Average deficiency percentage of the above 5 drivers	−28.28 %	−20.20 %	−67.78 %	−43.84 %	−20.47 %

of the four individual capitals for each country; (3) highlight NIC turning points, details of the enhancing or impeding factors, and the dynamics of factor changes for each country; and (4) calculate the distance that each country has to progress in order to achieve the benchmark GDP and identify the first five key factors to reach this goal. This section supplements the previous sections by looking into the contribution of each individual indicator in each year, rather than from the perspective of average scores and average rankings.

In this chapter, we reported our research findings in layman terms with graphs and tables of various types for easier reading. This study on national intangible assets has uncovered some important findings that are not apparent in other GDP-related studies. For instance, the average distance of the first five efficiency drivers to the same targeted GDP (Switzerland's) for Sweden (−20.47 %) is farther than that of Finland (−20.20 %), even though Sweden had better tangible and intangible performance than Finland. Although the difference is minute, it still conveys an important message for Sweden to ponder on.

Chapter 4
Beyond the 2008 Global Financial Crisis

This chapter reports activities after 2010, a time line regarded as the aftermath of the 2008 global financial crisis which was formally announced to be over at the end of 2009 (Kehoe, 2010; OECD, 2010). Although some European countries were still in sovereign debt trouble after 2010 (Greece requested another bailout in early 2012 and Spain asked for external financial assistance in June 2012), we use 2010 as a cutoff point in order to be consistent with the reports of other country clusters in this booklet series. From the statistics reported in Chaps. 2 and 3, economic situations of the Nordic countries (except Iceland) began to recover at the last quarter of 2009 under the support of government stimulus efforts and their relatively resilient financial systems after the early 1990s Nordic banking crisis.

The global financial turmoil of 2008 has not left the economies of these five countries unscathed, yet most of their economy rebounded faster than other advanced countries. Comfortable foreign exchange reserves and prudent financial practices allow these countries (except Iceland) to withstand the crisis. According to European Commission, discretionary stimulus measures of Sweden, Denmark, and Finland in 2009 and 2010 were in the range of 0.7–2.7 % of their GDP (Lindvall, 2011).

The initial notion that the relatively wealthy Nordic countries could decouple from the US subprime mortgage problems has proven wrong. Iceland was first hard-hit with their overexpanding financial markets across national borders. When the international market money dried up, Icelandic financial institutions were paralyzed leading to the government taking over the three largest banks. Iceland's financial disaster spilt over to its neighboring countries, including Finland, Norway, and Sweden. In addition, the vicious cycle of worldwide bankruptcies, job loss, reduced consumption, lost confidence, stalled financial activities, and drastically dropped export demands concurrently dragged the economy into unexpected crisis.

As a result, the foreign trade-dependent Nordic countries were all hit by the 2008 global financial crisis. Fortunately, with solid international reserves, sound financial systems, prudent financial practices after their early 1990s crisis, and the governments' swift actions, the Nordic countries had experienced rather fast recovery. Even Iceland is gradually picking up its economic development path.

C.Y.-Y. Lin et al., *National Intellectual Capital and the Financial Crisis in Denmark, Finland, Iceland, Norway, and Sweden*, SpringerBriefs in Economics,
DOI 10.1007/978-1-4614-9536-9_4,

Based on the World Economic Forum 2011–2012 report, worldwide recovery appeared fairly certain at the beginning of 2011 (Schwab, 2011). However in September 2011, OECD reported that major economies were tilting back into recession as sovereign debt problems continued to ail the Euro zone (Bryant, 2011). Concerns about the fiscal and banking problems continue to weigh on the global economic outlook, and economic activity contracted further in Europe (Reserve Bank of Australia [RBA], 2012).

In the first half of 2013, positive signs showed again. The International Monetary Fund (2013) reported that global prospects have improved, but the road of recovery in the advanced economies remained bumpy. For Nordic countries, the prospect is positive. Nordea (2013) projected 1.2 % and 2.0 % in economic growth for 2013 and 2014, respectively, up from 1.0 % growth in 2012.

In what follows, in the sequence of Denmark, Finland, Iceland, Norway, and Sweden, we briefly describe the economic status of these five countries after 2010 and their main causes of recovery.

Denmark

Denmark has recovered from this global financial crisis in 2010. Yet, the path of its recovery was not as fast and comprehensive as its neighboring countries. Denmark's most recent Global Competitiveness Index (ranked number 8) reported by World Economic Forum has not returned to its precrisis status (ranked number 4 in 2005) (Fig. 1.1). Its unemployment rate in 2010 (7.52 %) was still higher than that in 2005 (4.98 %) (Fig. 2.3). Our research also reveals that Denmark's national intellectual capital is losing its international competitiveness after the financial crisis (Table 3.2). The above situation agreed with the 2009 OECD report that Denmark's recovery might be slowed by the sizeable loss in competitiveness accumulated over the past few years due to strong wage growth and its exchange rate appreciation (OECD, 2009).

In retrospect, Carstensen (2011) summarized three main causes of Denmark's being caught in this financial crisis, including relaxed credit policies that led to an unsustainable level of deposit deficit in the banks, a boom in house prices, and an over-expansive fiscal policy. Several reasons also contributed to the country's recovery, other than the Danish government's timely coping measures. First, Denmark had maintained a healthy budget surplus for many years up to 2008, which facilitated Denmark modest recovery in 2010 in part because of increased government spending (Central Intelligence Agency [CIA], 2011). Second, Denmark has a long-standing stability-oriented economic policy with a focus on medium-term objectives, structural reforms, and labor market reform (Bernstein, 2010), which had built a solid foundation for economic progress. Third, Denmark enforced some policies after the crisis, including a strengthened mandate to dismiss managers and board members who mismanaged their banks with lax credit policies; strengthened power to commission an investigation by an external actor paid for by the financial institution being scrutinized; and issued a mandate to intervene in financial institutions in trouble at an earlier stage than was previously possible (Carstensen, 2011). Fourth, Danish government ensured the confidence in Danish banks with good timing and determination (Bernstein, 2010). Fifth, an important turning point was the stabilization of its currency "krone" in late October 2008. The currency stabilization had enabled Denmark to buy back foreign exchange and large-scale buybacks took place from early November 2008 (Bernstein). Sixth, in October 2010 the government introduced Bank Package III and doubled the deposit guarantee from around US$70,000 (€50,000) to US$140,000 (€100,000), pushing for further development and orderly winding up the destitute banks (Carstensen, 2011).

In 2010, Denmark was in a much better financial position; its foreign exchange reserve has exceeded around US$74.8 billion (DKK 400 billion) (Bernstein, 2010). The government was also working to achieve Denmark's 2015 fiscal targets by bringing the structural budget balance back. In addition, the 2011 elected prime minister has pledged to increase government spending, raise taxes on the wealthy, and adopt an unusual plan to make everyone work 12 minutes more per day for an extra hour each week (RTE News, 2011). These are promising measures for Denmark to regain its economic strength.

For the 2013 economic outlook, Nordea (2013) reported that Denmark would be under pressure due to the waning activity in its neighboring German, Swedish, and British markets; in addition, the country would experience late labor market turnaround. However, its housing market has shown signs of improvement with prices up, and the rising disposable incomes and a gradual pickup in economic activity globally might get Danish household consumption out of the doldrums.

Finland

Finland has experienced a relatively strong recovery, compared with other Nordic countries. Although its 2011–2012 Global Competitiveness Index (ranked number 4) reported by the World Economic Forum has not yet returned to its precrisis status (ranked number 1 in 2005) (Fig. 1.1), other indices all showed very positive signs. In terms of the real GDP growth, Finland was impacted by this financial crisis the most among the Nordic countries. In 2009, its real GDP growth was down to −8.65 %; yet, in 2010, the growth was bounced back to positive 2.63 % almost similar to its 2005 level (Fig. 2.1) and achieved 2.9 % and 0.6 % growth in 2011 and 2012, respectively (Global Finance, 2013a). Its general government debt, unemployment rate, and consumer price inflation all returned to its 2005 status after the financial crisis. Our research also reveals that Finland's national intellectual capital has gained its international competitiveness after the financial crisis, particularly in market capital and process capital (Table 3.2), even though there were score decreases.

In Western Europe, Finland was among the hardest hit by this crisis (Juel, 2011). Fortunately, Finnish banks faced the 2008 global financial turbulence in a relatively healthy condition for several reasons. First, the solvency of all Finnish banks exceeded the statutory requirement of 8 %; second, regulation and management of the Finnish banking sector was much more sophisticated than during the previous financial crisis in the early 1990s; third, the banking sector was marked by a renewed sense of caution after the 1990s experience; fourth, internal risk procedures, such as the criteria for corporate and private lending, were tightened after the 1990s; and fifth, enterprises were closely monitored by banks (Tervanen, 2009). Particularly, after Finland's crisis in the early 1990s, it enacted many reforms, such as setting fiscal rules that the budget should be in surplus during an economic cycle, tightened the regulation and surveillance of banks, and requested banks' self-initiated risk management (Juel, 2011). These efforts had resulted in a gradual reduction in government debt after the mid-1990s and a resilient financial system. Finland is also the only Economic and Monetary Union (EMU) country that has never violated the EMU budget rule of deficit not exceeding 3 % of GDP (Juel, 2011). These preconditions have made Finnish banks more resilient to the external impact. Unlike many banks in other European countries, Finnish banks did not need government support during this crisis (Tervanen, 2009).

In 2010, a recovery of exports, domestic trade, household consumption, and ongoing fiscal stimulus facilitated Finland's economic growth (CIA, 2011; OECD, 2010). As a result, GDP stopped falling and signs of a turnaround were emerging (OECD, 2010). The 2010 deficit in Finland at 2.7 % of GDP was much better than the OECD average of 5.6 %. Finland also kept its expenditure ceilings in place with its positive structural balance in 2010 (OECD, 2010). Even after running deficits in 2009 and 2010, gross debt (around 48 %) in Finland was well below the OECD average at 57.4 % of GDP in 2010 (OECD, 2010).

In the budget for 2011, Finnish government announced that there would be a transition from expansionary to restrictive (contractive) fiscal policies, and the temporary stimulus measures would be phased out gradually, as in the other Nordic countries (Lindvall, 2011). Although the Finnish banks were not severely impacted by this global financial crisis, the crisis has affected the Finnish banking sector in another respect by leading to structural changes regarding monetary financial institutions (Tervanen, 2009). Such influence will help further improve the Finnish financial system.

In June 2013, Nordea (2013) reported that Finland's economy was stalled by the lasting recession in the Euro area, slower economic growth in Russia and China. According to Nordea's forecast, in 2013, exports would remain subdued, investment would decrease, employment would continue to weaken, consumer price growth would slow down, trade balance would show a small surplus, and the government's borrowing need would continue to be significant with the public debt to GDP ratio approaching 60 % at a steady pace.

Iceland

Iceland is slowly emerging from a deep recession following the collapse of its three largest banks. Although its most recent Global Competitiveness Index (ranked number 30) reported by World Economic Forum shows a sharp decline comparing to its precrisis status (ranked number 7 in 2005) (Fig. 1.1), there were signs of gradual recovery. Iceland's real GDP growth was down to −8.06 % in 2009; yet, in 2010, it improved to −3.17 % (Fig. 2.1). Its consumer price inflation was reduced to 5.4 % in 2010 from 12.04 % in 2009 (Fig. 2.4). Iceland's economy stopped contracting by late 2010. The primary general government budget deficit was up to 6.9 % of GDP in 2009, yet cut to 2.8 % of GDP in 2010 (OECD, 2011b).

Both Iceland's internal determination and external assistance had helped the country to its gradual recovery. The turnaround was mainly attributable to several reasons (OECD, 2011b). First, in November 2008, Iceland agreed a comprehensive program named Stand-By Arrangement (SBA) with the IMF, aiming to restore its financial sector to health, return its public finances to sustainability, prevent capital flight by capital controls, and rebuild monetary policy credibility by stabilizing inflation at low levels. SBA's major programs included a medium-term fiscal consolidation, involving painful austerity measures and significant tax hikes; a viable but sharply downsized domestic banking system; and the enactment of capital controls with the timetable of gradual control lift to restore financial linkages with the outside world.

Second, Icelandic banking system was recapitalized by the end of 2009. Reforms had been made to the regulation and supervision concerning shortcomings exposed by the financial crisis. The Central Bank of Iceland (CBI) and the Financial Supervisory Authority (FSA) signed a cooperation agreement to strengthen macroprudential supervision. Third, the revival of export growth and sharp contraction in imports due to reduced domestic demand contributed to the turnaround. Fourth, the large real exchange rate depreciation had also helped stabilize Iceland's economic system and was a main factor explaining Iceland's decline in inflation.

Fifth, steps had been taken to accelerate private-sector debt restructuring. The government and financial institutions had signed a nonbinding agreement to accelerate debt restructuring for viable SMEs (OECD, 2010). Financial institutions reform had given management a mandate for restructuring nonperforming loans and for necessary capital information to support debt write-downs. To restrain future buildup of systemic risks, interactions between the macro- and microprudential supervision had also been noted (Carey, 2009). By the end of 2010, Iceland had completed the restructuring of most of the afflicted financial institutions. Sixth, the SBA's program had helped the country from being seriously affected by the 2010 European sovereign debt crisis.

Up to 2011, Iceland has fulfilled the main conditions in each of its IMF SBA reviews; consequently, the SBA program was scheduled to conclude in August 2011 (OECD, 2011b). The authorities also released a strategy for the removal of capital controls, which was an important factor in rebuilding trust with international investors and enabling Icelandic companies to access global capital markets. Compared to some of the countries still struggling in the Euro zone, Iceland was in a relatively good place in 2011 (Phillips, 2011). Another sign of the success of Iceland's efforts was that the Icelandic government was able to raise US$1 billion with a bond issue in June 2011. This development indicated that international investors had given Iceland and its new banking system a clean bill of health (Ward, 2011).

Although Iceland's general government debt was still high at 120 % of its GDP in 2010 (Fig. 2.2) and our research revealed that Iceland was losing its international competitiveness in almost every type of national intellectual capital (Table 3.2), its coming back to the international market is apparent. Some good signs include Iceland has actually achieved a real GDP growth of 3.1 % in 2011 and 2.4 % in 2012 (Global Finance, 2013a), rather than its earlier prediction of 1 % in 2011 (OECD, 2011b). In addition, its deficit has been reduced from −6.4 % (2010), −4.6 % (2011) to −2.8 % (2012) and unemployment rate reduced from 8.1 % (2010), 7.4 % (2011) to 6.3 % (2012) (Global Finance, 2013a). The above report has painted a promising picture for Iceland's future.

Norway

Norway recovered from the 2008 global financial crisis the fastest among the Nordic countries. Although its 2011–2012 Global Competitiveness Index (ranked number 16) reported by World Economic Forum has not yet returned to its precrisis status (ranked number 9 in 2005) (Fig. 1.1), other indicators all show very positive signs. In terms of the real GDP growth, Norway was still impacted by this financial crisis, irrespective to its wealth. In 2009, its real GDP growth was down to −2.70 %, the least affected among the Nordic countries (Fig. 2.1). Its general government debt was relatively stable during the financial crisis (Fig. 2.2); unemployment rate of 3.6 % in 2010 was the lowest among the group with an improvement from 4.6 % in 2005; its consumer price inflation was also relatively low at 2.5 % in 2010. Our research revealed that Norway's national intellectual capital gained its international competitiveness after the financial crisis, particularly in market capital (Table 3.2).

In October 2008, an acute situation with lack of bank liquidity occurred, and bank loan losses increased during 2009. Yet, the problems were quickly resolved by the joint measures of Norges Bank, the central bank, and Norwegian government. In addition, the substantial government stimuli both in autumn 2008 and winter 2009 had a profound effect. The major reasons that contributed to Norway's fast recovery can be summarized as follows:

First, Norway has sound financial systems. The resilience of the Norwegian banking system was a result of lessons learned after the Nordic banking crisis in the early 1990s. Ever since, the risk management systems in banks were strongly improved and remained well in place prior to this financial crisis (Halvorsen, 2009; Juel, 2011). A prudent and long-term-oriented economic policy was also an important contributor. Since 1994, Kredittilsynet (Financial Supervisory Authority of Norway) has analyzed and assessed potential stability problems in the Norwegian financial industry, based on Norwegian and international economic development (Kredittilsynet, 2009). Second, the accumulation of assets from hydrocarbon production in Norway's National Wealth Fund had provided a cushion for fiscal stimulus (CIA, 2011; Juel, 2011; Kredittilsynet, 2009). Fortunately, the petroleum market remained rather stable during 2009, despite the downturn of the world economy, thus stabilizing Norway's economy. As a result, the Norwegian government's financial room for maneuver was large and the policy reactions were strong (Juel, 2011).

Third, Norway is not highly dependent on consumer goods exports. While manufacturing production in the Euro area was down more than 20 % in the first 4 months of 2009 compared to the same period in 2008, the decline in Norway was a mere 6 % (Halvorsen, 2009). Fourth, although house prices were elevated, no housing bubble burst (Juel, 2011). Norway's prudent financial system had protected their banks' exposure to the toxic assets (Halvorsen, 2009).

Fifth, learning from their experience in the early 1990s, the Norwegian government intervened very early to prevent the confidence fall, such as interest rate cuts, improved market liquidity, and recapitalized financial institutions (Kredittilsynet, 2009). Kredittilsynet knew that the government supplied banks with equity capital through the Finance Fund was very important to stabilize the economy. Sixth, Norway also benefited from many years of integrated financial supervision and legislation covering the entire financial market. Individual institutions' profitability and financial strength need to be carried out against the backdrop of the general state of the financial system. Furthermore, such assessment of the financial market has been published since 2003, which provides transparent information to ensure financial stability (Kredittilsynet, 2009).

In addition to internal coping measures, the Norwegian government also contributed its experiences to help EU work out a sound framework for the financial markets internationally, so that other countries could also underpin a prosperous and sustainable development for the world economy in the years to come (Halvorsen, 2009).

For 2013 economic outlook, Nordea (2013) predicted that business investment in Norway would still be subdued, purchasing power growth would be low, labor market weakening, and wage growth and inflation remain low as well.

Sweden

Sweden experienced relatively good recovery, even though it was much harder hit by this global financial crisis due to its heavy reliance on consumer goods production. The most positive sign was its 2011–2012 Global Competitiveness Index (ranked number 3) reported by World Economic Forum has returned to its precrisis status (also ranked number 3 in 2005) (Fig. 1.1). Other indicators are also very positive indicating its strong recovery. In terms of the real GDP growth, Sweden did show a negative impact by this financial crisis, down to −5.88 % in 2009 yet rebounded to positive 5.04 % in 2010 (Fig. 2.1). Its general government debt was relatively stable and low during the financial crisis with 39.76 % in 2010 (Fig. 2.2). The unemployment rate was relatively high compared to other Nordic countries and rose from 7.3 % in 2005 to 8.4 % in 2010. However, such unemployment is considered modest comparing to other EU countries. Sweden's consumer price inflation was very low at 1.17 % in 2010. Our research also revealed that Sweden's national intellectual capital has gained international competitiveness after the financial crisis, particularly in market capital and process capital (Table 3.2).

In November 2009, the first signs of recovery were observable in Sweden (Jochem, 2010). As reported above, the debt buildup has been small. According to Swedish government projections, the automatic strengthening of the budget following the closing of the output gap would be sufficient to restore a public surplus in 2013 (Hassler, 2010). A US Congressional Research Service reported that Sweden was a successful model about how to cope with a financial crisis (Nanto, 2009).

Several reasons contributed to Sweden's recovery from this financial crisis. First, strong exports of commodities and a return to profitability by Sweden's banking sector drove the strong rebound in 2010 (CIA, 2011). Second, the comprehensive and clearly formulated stabilization measures for the financial system were designed and implemented fast enough. The active measures taken to stabilize the banking sector and the emphasis on protecting taxpayer money increased confidence in financial institutions (Jochem, 2010). Third, Sweden entered the crisis with a surplus of 3.5 % GDP in 2007, while the average of EU, USA, and Japan was negative. In addition, its net financial position was positive at 18 % of GDP in the beginning of 2008 (Hassler, 2010).

Fourth, this global financial crisis did not trigger a Swedish domestic financial crisis. After the early 1990s Nordic crisis, Sweden had enacted many reforms, including fiscal rules that the budget should be in surplus during an economic cycle, requested banks' own risk management, and the regulation of banks and surveillance were also improved (Juel, 2011). As a result, the Swedish financial system has become more resilient. Fifth, there was an increase in central government grants to local governments (Jochem, 2010), which helped to disburse the stimulus money in a more efficient manner. Sixth, major stimulus measures are integrated into the budget, which could increase the resources allocated and prolong the stimulus effect. For example, investment in transportation infrastructure focusing on maintenance works and expanding the public transportation system was approximately 3.4 % of GDP in the 2009–2011 period. Stabilization measures were applied to Sweden's car industry, including around US$0.42 billion (SEK 3 billion) in research and development funds for the auto industry and loan guarantees worth around US$2.8 billion (SEK 20 billion) for developing green technologies also in the car industry (Jochem). In the 2010 budget (passed in September 2009), the government further increased spending.

For 2013 economic outlook, Sweden's prospect is better than other Nordic countries, mainly driven by stronger consumer spending. Specifically, its exports that declined at the beginning of 2013 were expected to improve in the latter part of the year; rising wages and low inflation have boosted households' purchasing power; furthermore, 2014 is an election year with income tax expected to be lowered for boosting household spending power (Nordea, 2013). In addition, Swedish government's expansionary fiscal policy, public spending, and increased investment will help the economy as well.

Chapter 5
Future Perspectives and Policy Implications

By the middle of 2013, more than 4 years have passed since the outbreak of the 2008 global financial crisis. Although some countries in the European Union are still in financial trouble, it is time to reflect upon what happened during the past few years and what can be learned from this crisis for future prevention.

Signs of recovery started to show at the end of 2009 in the Nordic countries, and recovery was pretty certain in 2010 with Iceland at a slower pace starting 2011. However, world economy was stagnated again in the second half of 2011, mainly due to sovereign debt problems in Europe and a modest recovery in the USA. In January 2012, the IMF announced that the global recovery was threatened by intensifying strains in the Euro area; thus, financial conditions have deteriorated, growth prospects have dimmed, and downside risks have escalated (International Monetary Fund [IMF], 2012). The Euro area economy went into a mild recession in 2012. The effects of bank deleveraging on the real economy surfaced again and the impact of additional fiscal consolidation heightened. Even growth in developing economies that had traditionally remained resilient slowed down because of the worsening external environment and a weakening of internal demand (IMF, 2012).

Although World Bank (2012) projected only 2.5 % growth for 2012, statistics of January 2013 showed that the world economy in 2012 grew by 3.7 %, with Euro area 0.7 %, advanced countries 2 %, and developing Asia 8.1 % (Global Finance, 2013b). In April 2013, IMF (2013) reported that global prospects have improved. In the major advanced economies, activity was expected to gradually accelerate with the USA taking the lead. World output growth was predicted to reach 3.25 % in 2013 and 4 % in 2014. For Nordic countries, Nordea (2013) projected 1.2 % and 2.0 % of economic growth for 2013 and 2014, respectively, up from 1.0 % growth in 2012. These numbers reveal that in the years to come, there are promising prospects as well as challenges that need world leaders to pay close attention.

In this chapter, we first present the prospects of these five Nordic countries and then describe their potential challenges in the future. The prospects and challenges are meant to provide points of thought for discussion and do not represent an exhaustive list. This chapter finishes with some policy implications.

C.Y.-Y. Lin et al., *National Intellectual Capital and the Financial Crisis in Denmark, Finland, Iceland, Norway, and Sweden*, SpringerBriefs in Economics,
DOI 10.1007/978-1-4614-9536-9_5, © The Author(s) 2014

Prospects

From the above report, most of the Nordic countries embedded their national medium-term or long-term goal to their stimulus package for future national development, along with resolving pressing financial issues. As each individual country has its own systems and resources, we briefly describe the prospects of each country as follows.

Denmark

After the financial crisis, a promising future in Denmark is the stipulation of new policies which give Danish Financial Supervisory Authority (FSA) the discretion to exercise its power for establishing more effective financial systems (Carstensen, 2011). The crisis thus created a window of opportunity to establish a new and more aggressive supervision of Danish banks (Carstensen, 2011). The new law represents a marked institutional change and a reorganization of the relationship between the state and the financial sector for serving the purposes of enhancing the possibility of the FSA to intervene at an earlier stage, increasing the level of information disclosure about financial institutions, and delimiting the legitimate type of banking business in the financial sector.

Specifically, a "supervision diamond" was designed to regulate five value limits: the sum of large engagements should be less than 125 % of base capital, growth in lending should be less than 20 % per year, exposure to the building industry should be less than 25 % of total lending, stable funding based on lending/capital ratio should be less than one, and a requirement of more than 50 % liquidity over the minimum liquidity demand (Carstensen, 2011). A financial institution that exceeds one or more of the value limits will be considered having an unsound business model and will be under scrutiny. With the new policy, credit institutions are also obliged to publish the FSA's risk assessments, criticisms, and orders.

In addition, the FSA also evaluates soft criteria that are not measurable through accounting figures, for example, issues of (mis)management. If the FSA senses that the management is not in control of the situation or is not following the approved credit policy of the institution, the supervisory diamond will be used to determine when the FSA should intervene (Carstensen, 2011). Actually, the new law requires that the FSA must intervene when it seems likely that a financial institution may lose its license in the shorter or longer term, without the institution necessarily violating any laws.

The exercise of this new law has resulted in the dismiss of six directors of Danish financial institutions between its implementation in July 2010 and February 2011 and has brought fifteen individuals previously affiliated with the bank (e.g., the director, board members, and an auditor) to trial for breach of fiduciary trust (Carstensen, 2011). The new policies and ensuing actions have clearly shown

Denmark's determination for financial structural reforms, which should help establish a more resilient national economy in the future.

Finland

Although Finland has been hit hard by this financial crisis, it has recovered relatively well from our report in previous sections. For future development, the following strengths Finland has accumulated over the decades may help the country sustain its competitiveness.

First, Finnish banking sector is stable, which will help support its national development. During the crisis, the solid profitability and capital adequacy buffers have enabled Finnish banking and lending operations to continue functioning (Tervanen, 2009). This provides a good proof of its resilience from external impact. Second, Finnish regional development policy will support its future national development. Regional development, such as Helsinki region, has been planned by the government and will help boost housing investment, infrastructure investment, and talent enrichment. Third, Finland has led its economy with a strong emphasis on R&D and innovation after it was recovered from the early 1990s Nordic banking crisis (Lin, 2009). Such strategy has helped attract and retain high-quality human resources and becomes the backbone of its economic development. Fourth, Finland invests heavily in education and talent development. According to World Economic Forum report, Finland occupies the top position in the higher education and training pillar, which has laid the groundwork for high levels of technological adoption and innovation (Palkamo, 2011). In Finland, students benefit from grants and allowances that are both generous and virtually open ended (OECD, 2010). In addition, Finland's students PISA performance is the highest in Europe. Qualified human resource is a valuable asset for Finland.

With these strengths, Finland is standing firm for a continuous recovery and future development.

Iceland

Iceland's financial disaster was mainly caused by the micro-mismanagement of the banking sector, amplified to the macro level. Now that the worse is over, the following features may help the country pick up its growth again. First, after the crisis, steps have been taken to reduce future risk. Measures contain excluding cross-linked loans from collateral eligible for central bank loans, setting up a register for large borrowers, strengthening audit requirements, adopting the most comprehensive Basel III framework, and signing a cooperation agreement between the Central Bank of Iceland and the Financial Supervisory Authority in early 2011 to allow better identification of common risks across institutions (OECD, 2011b).

Second, Iceland's strong rule of law, low levels of corruption, and competitive tax rates remain solid foundations on which to build recovery and restore economic stability (Heritage Foundation, 2012). If reinforced by further financial management reforms, these features will generate very good effects. Third, during the financial crisis, additional funds were made available to all persons seeking to complete their secondary education. In addition, vocational programs were further developed, training classes were made more relevant, and the highly successful long-term internship program was expanded (OECD, 2011b). These measures help upgrade the quality of Icelandic human resources. Fourth, energy resources are to be developed subject to environmental constraints. Iceland has large amounts of low-cost geothermal and hydroelectric energy and considerable scope to develop it further, which could provide a significant boost to long-run economic growth (OECD).

The opposite side of disaster is a turning point. Iceland has been going through financial difficulties for several years. Yet, with internal structural reforms and external assistance, new policies and new resources bring new hopes. The above stated features should play a role in facilitating Iceland's future prospects.

Norway

Norway is the least affected Nordic country in this financial crisis, which gives the country a head start for future development. The following features may provide Norway the strength for its next stage of development. First, Norway keeps its wealth for future generations to come. In anticipation of eventual declines in oil and gas production, Norway saves state revenue from the petroleum sector in the world's second largest sovereign wealth fund, valued at over US$500 billion in 2010 (Central Intelligence Agency [CIA], 2011). Second, Norway has fully utilized its national wealth to meet future challenge. Its Pension Fund – Global has invested in financial assets abroad to ensure that future generations may take part in the petroleum wealth (Halvorsen, 2009). Third, Norway is prudent in financial management and only spends the expected real return from the fund over the annual budgets. Such practice contributes to stabilizing the Norwegian economy. Fourth, entrepreneurial activity is well supported by prudent and transparent regulations governing investment and the financial sector. Together with openness to global commerce, strong protection of property rights also supports economic dynamism. Norway's high level of business freedom has produced a commercial environment that is both innovative and resilient (Heritage Foundation, 2012). With these features, Norway can step up its future development.

Sweden

Sweden was also hard-hit by this financial crisis, yet its fast recovery and effective public finances management during the crisis has gained substantial international attention (Hassler, 2010). The following features may help Sweden advance further in the future. First, Sweden differs from many OECD countries in regard to low corruption, high trust embedded in Swedish society, as well as a highly educated labor force (Jochem, 2010). Second, the spirit of unity will have a profound impact on Sweden's development. Despite political competition, from the beginning of this crisis, broad political unity between government and opposition has been achieved. Such unity enables the government to combine crisis measures with political goals to strengthen Sweden's international competitiveness. Third, Sweden emphasizes the education of the rising generation. During this financial crisis, it also applied the stimulus funds to education, increasing the amount dedicated to student loans and investing in vocational training outside the framework of active labor market policies. This implies increased numbers of places for students in the regular (municipal) education system. Around US$0.32 billion (SEK 2.3 billion) in 2010 and US$0.31 billion (SEK 2.2 billion) in 2011 was allocated in support of an education stimulus (Jochem, 2010). Other matching funds are also in place up to 2012. Fourth, Sweden is taking the opportunity of this financial crisis to enhance its ongoing structural change.

Solid fundamentals, new resources, and ongoing reforms should lead to a promising future for Sweden.

Challenges

Despite the relative fast recovery of the Nordic countries (except Iceland) from the financial crisis, they still face some challenges that may hamper future development. This section, while not exhaustive, lists some of the challenges for readers' reference and exploration.

Denmark

Denmark is historically a large welfare state, which is strongly supported by the people. Yet, some issues began to surface as time goes by. First, tax burden have become an issue. Although Danish corporate tax rate is competitive, the overall tax burden remains heavy (48.7 %, the highest in the EU), which posits an increasing concern as its burden on the overall economy becomes more difficult to sustain (Economic Freedom, 2011). Second, an aging workforce has become a concern (CIA, 2011). Among the five Nordic countries, Denmark is third in terms of elderly citizens. The ratio of 65 years old and over is higher than that of Iceland and Norway. Although aging is becoming a common threat to advanced countries, coping measures need to be planned as early as possible. Third, labor productivity needs to be further enhanced. After the financial crisis, the employment rate is now among the highest in the OECD. However, while labor utilization has been growing, productivity has slowed. As a result, national income per capita has lost ground vis-à-vis the leading OECD economies (OECD, 2009). Fourth, to boost productivity, pursuing an agenda focused on productivity-enhancing reforms in education and the business sector is needed (OECD, 2009). Fifth, although the Financial Supervisory Authority (FSA) was handed the power to implement the new regulation set during the financial crisis, its success relies on whether the FSA has the means to put the new regulation to use effectively (Carstensen, 2011).

Finland

Finland is hard-hit by this financial crisis mainly because of high dependence on exports goods. After its recovery, there are some challenges that may impede its future development. First, the recession has left a deep mark on general government finances and the debt ratio. Despite good growth prospects, general government finances will remain in a deficit for the next few years (CIA, 2011). Second, a great challenge of Finland's economic policy is to implement a postrecession exit strategy. To better utilize the resources, it will be important to combine measures supporting continuous growth with general budget adjustment in the wake of the crisis. Third, an aging workforce is a great concern. The median age of Finland is the largest among the five Nordic countries. Longer term, Finland must address the issue of a rapidly aging population and decreasing productivity that threaten competitiveness, fiscal sustainability, and economic growth.

Fourth, restrictive labor regulations undermine employment and productivity growth (Economic Freedom, 2011). Finland needs to reconsider its labor regulations to cope with its aging population and shrinking workforce to maintain future growth and its generous social spending programs. Fifth, fast rising unit labor costs has lowered Finland's competitiveness. High wage increases and an appreciating effective exchange rate have deteriorated competitiveness over the last few years, potentially denting Finland's export performance (OECD, 2010). Sixth, the interface between the secondary and tertiary education needs to be improved. Many high school graduates are forced to wait extended periods before obtaining a place at a university due to entry exams, in addition to a standardized exit test at the secondary level (OECD, 2010). Seventh, overreliance on one large company (Nokia) for national development may pose a future threat. Powell (2011) cited a quotation from Pekka Yla-Anttila of the Research Institute of the Finnish Economy, saying "I don't think you can find any other developed industrial economy where one company has played such a big role." To release this potential threat, Finland needs to turn positive attitudes and investments into entrepreneurial activity, as it is rated significantly behind most of its European and all of its Scandinavian counterparts (Powell). Eighth, Finland needs to widen and deepen its knowledge economy in competing with the low tax and low wage in some EU countries (Lin, 2009).

Iceland

With Iceland's collapsed financial system, its route to full economic recovery will be much longer than other countries. Yet, it is also a good opportunity for Iceland to adopt more fundamental reforms along the recovering process. If attending to the following issues, its regaining competitiveness can be anticipated.

First, Iceland's monetary policy framework needs to be strengthened. The policy has not been very effective either in countering the credit cycle or in delivering price stability (OECD, 2010). An important challenge is to ensure that Iceland has monetary policy institutions that are effective in delivering price stability, especially after capital controls are lifted. To improve performance, the Central Bank of Iceland should adopt an inflation-targeting regime that places greater weight on smoothing fluctuations in the exchange rate and is supported by fiscal policy and macroprudential regulation. Furthermore, in the past the banks relied too much on wholesale funding, which tends to be less stable than retail deposits and dried up as concerns about the banks' solvency grew (OECD, 2010).

Second, challenges to the fisheries management system need to be addressed in a way that preserves a sustainable and efficient fishery. Iceland has been successful in managing its large fishing industry with its systems of Total Allowable Catches based on scientific recommendations and the Individual Quota System. Yet, this system could be threatened by potential policy responses to the perceived unfairness of quotas initially having been given away (OECD, 2011b). Icelandic government may need to increase the special resource tax on fishing to a level that neither causes financial difficulties in the industry nor destroys the quota system (OECD, 2011).

Third, it is difficult for Iceland to attract foreign direct investment (FDI) due to the currency arrangements. There is high financing cost due to the small currency (Phillips, 2011). In addition, around 90 % of the resources used in power production are owned by national or subnational governments, and an OECD ranking puts Iceland as one of the least open member countries to FDI. It is suggested to revise the FDI law to clarify the authorities' scope for action and to reduce uncertainty (OECD, 2011b). Electricity problems are also a barrier to FDI.

Fourth, although Iceland began accession negotiations with the EU in July 2010, there is a great concern about losing control over fishing resources (CIA, 2011; Phillips, 2011). Joining the Euro area would significantly lower the volatility of traded good prices and lower overall inflation volatility as nearly half of Iceland's external trade is with countries in the Euro area or pegged to it (Central Bank of Iceland [CBI], 2010). In addition, the reduction in the inflation risk premium and the elimination of the exchange rate risk premium with respect to the Euro would lower domestic real interest rates, fostering higher capital intensity and increasing productivity (OECD, 2010). Yet, Icelanders did not want to commit themselves to the EU until they have a clear understanding of how it will affect their fishing fleet (Phillips, 2011). The issue of whether to be integrated to the EU system needs to be carefully handled.

Fifth, the government should target assistance for housing costs more tightly on lower-income households and should deliver it through measures that do not accord policy-related competitive advantages to the Housing Financing Fund as they reduce the efficiency of financial intermediation services and expose the taxpayer to financial risks (OECD, 2010). Sixth, implementing private-sector debt restructuring will lay a solid foundation for future economic growth. Measures need to be taken and accelerated in assisting economic recovery. Seventh, geothermal and particularly hydroelectric power raises considerable environmental concerns, which must be dealt with on a project-by-project basis (OECD, 2011b).

Norway

During this financial crisis, Norway fared well with its sound financial systems and abundant reserves. Yet, challenges still lie ahead to achieve its long-term sustainability. First, preserving economic competitiveness will be a future concern (CIA, 2011). Norway's overall strong record of economic freedom is marred by high levels of government spending and the privatization agenda has also stalled (Economic Freedom, 2011). Second, sound banking system needs to be reassured. If Norwegian banks' access to funding in international markets is to be assured, their high standard capital adequacy level needs to be strengthened. Banks must therefore, as far as possible, endeavor to assure sufficient equity capital through continued profitability (Kredittilsynet, 2009).

Third, the residual problems of the stimulus package need to be dealt with. The authorities may face a very difficult situation in the aftermath of the financial crisis; intervention by the authorities on short notice in so many areas of the economy is problematic. Problems also include supplying substantial volumes of liquidity which could lay the basis for higher inflation in the longer term, the government takeover of banks may also have an unintended effect on competitive conditions in the country's banking sector, and measures taken may give rise to undesirable conduct on the part of financial market actors (Kredittilsynet, 2009). In addition, there is a risk that the stimulus packages may contribute to the buildup of price bubbles in the government bond market. Moral-hazard problems may also be a concern. As a result, in the wake of the financial crisis the conduct of both monetary and fiscal policy will have to take account of new risk structures (Kredittilsynet, 2009).

Fourth, extensive market financing has proven very vulnerable and loan securitization needs to be distributed. Uncertainty about the distribution of risk and doubt about individual institutions' financial strength and liquidity position have developed into a threat to the financial system. Therefore, stricter requirements on information disclosure about the characteristics of financial instruments are needed to improve transparency and market discipline (Kredittilsynet, 2009).

Fifth, streaming the huge oil revenues into welfare gains is a challenge. Norwegian government continues to save a large portion of its hugely prosperous oil export revenues in investment funds outside of the country as insurance against depleting reserves (Economic Freedom, 2011). Yet, how to transform this fluctuating revenue stream into welfare gains for both current and future generations (Halvorsen, 2009) in the increasingly volatile environment is a challenge.

Sixth, other concerns include Norway's immigration and integration of ethnic minorities and how to maintain the country's extensive social safety net with an aging population (CIA, 2011).

Sweden

Sweden's coping measures to revive the economic during the financial crisis were effective. Although economically recovered, there are still challenges ahead as described hereunder. First, Sweden's main challenge going forward is to strengthen or renew institutions and fundamentals even further so as to keep enhancing resilience and sustainable long-term growth (Gurria, 2011). For instance, the central bank could improve communication to clarify the financial system's institutional framework and the allocation of responsibilities for ensuring well-designed and well-assigned regulations and toolkits (Gurria, 2011). Public sectors, such as the railroad, health services, and the educational system, may follow the similar renewal path.

Second, Sweden's highest risks are associated with the activities of Swedish banks in the Baltic states (Jochem, 2010). In contrast to the Nordic crisis in the early 1990s, the current financial crisis is international. Therefore, continuous attention to the development of the Baltic region and surrounding areas is necessary.

Third, increasing levels of unemployment, especially youth unemployment, will soon be one of the biggest political problems in Sweden (Jochem, 2010). There is a risk of a permanent increase in structural or regional unemployment. Sweden has consistently had the highest youth (age 15–29) unemployment rate in the five Nordic countries beginning in 2005, ranging from 14 % to 18 %. In 2010, youth unemployment in Sweden was around 18 %, compared to Denmark 13 %, Finland 16 %, Iceland 14 %, and Norway 7 % (Carlsen et al., 2011, p. 17). The EU promoted a "flexicurity" labor policy, combining flexibility and security (European Union [EU], 2013). This provides a good direction for reducing the youth unemployment problems. In addition, dealing with the temporary employment issues would foster the inclusion of groups at the margin of the labor market; also, improving the wage bargaining framework would ease labor market adjustments (Jochem, 2010).

Fourth, the efficiency of active labor market policies should be raised by increasing the use of competency training, targeting it toward those who need it the most. In addition, there should be more cooperation between institutions in raising the labor efficiency (Gurria, 2011). The German apprentice system has been lauded for enhancing youth skills as well as promoting their employability (Ewing, 2009; IPEZone, 2012)

Fifth, there was a call for R&D and universities reform. Sweden has a long tradition of investing generously in R&D as a high-ranking knowledge nation. However, during the last two decades, the development of research with high international impact has been weaker in Sweden than in countries such as Denmark, the Netherlands, and Switzerland (Oquist & Benner, 2012; Stjernlöf, 2013). Swedish universities did not perform at the same level as the universities in the reference countries, and university managements did not adequately prioritize the very highest international academic quality (Oquist & Benner; Stjernlöf). It is important for government to support free research inspired by bold and innovative ideas.

Sixth, further reforms of the social benefit and tax systems are needed to provide the right incentives for increasing hours worked (Gurria, 2011), to cope with the shrinking and aging labor force.

Seventh, the future of the public–private organizing mix of the service sectors will be very critical and strongly influenced by competition between the two political blocs (Jochem, 2010).

Policy Implications

Unexpectedly, what started off as a subprime mortgage problem in the USA triggered a widespread global financial crisis. Even the advanced Nordic countries reported in this volume were not immune from the impact. This event clearly evidences how interdependent and interconnected the world economies have become.

The causes of this financial crisis are multifaceted, including the much blamed high-risk financial products, undisclosed conflicts of interest, failure of regulation and the credit rating agencies. In addition, the sovereignty debt problem that broke out in the European Union region adds more complex dimensions to this crisis. The overliberation of the banking industry, the fragile financial system, and weak national governance surfaced all together at one time. It is a linking system breakdown that failed to withhold the impact of sudden financial shock.

Behind statistics, such as percentage GDP growth drop and export volume decrease, are the hidden intangibles – the people, systems, governance, market dynamics, and regulation flaws – that brought about this global financial catastrophe. NIC research reported in this booklet covers human capital, market capital, process capital, and renewal capital encompassing key intangible elements described above. Our data analysis uncovered individual national intangible assets as well as country cluster comparisons and provide valuable information for the policy makers to look back at the NIC before the crisis, observe the situation during the crisis, and study its progression afterward.

By investigating the economic development and NIC development spanning 2005–2010 at the same time, we have been able to draw the connection between the tangibles and the intangibles for these five countries. Some implications can be derived from our research findings as illustrated here under:

First, maintaining a sound financial system is an endless job to navigate and withstand future financial shock. The Nordic countries presented in this booklet recovered from the 2008 global financial crisis very well (except Iceland), mainly because of their sound financial systems reformed after the early 1990s Nordic crisis. After that crisis, their governments enacted many reforms, strengthened the regulation and surveillance of banks, and enforced the banks' own risk management. The banking sector as well as legislators and supervisory authorities had learned the true cost of imprudent risk-taking and insufficient credit evaluations. Relevant reforms had led to a stronger, more resilient, and disciplined financial system. Although still hit by this financial crisis, even the non-oil countries – Denmark, Finland, and Sweden – were able to recover faster than most of other advanced countries.

Studies of past financial crises uncover a pattern that financial crisis generally came about after a period of vigorous and persistent credit growth combined with sharply rising prices in real estate and securities markets. In the future, similar crisis is likely to occur. A single country may not be able to prevent a financial crisis from happening; yet at the least it can withstand it with a disciplined financial system and good national governance for a fast recovery, as the major Nordic countries did this time. Therefore, continuously examine financial fundamentals to institute necessary structural reforms is an endless job for building a more resilient economy.

Second, positioning in the international markets is a crucial strategic issue especially for small economies. Economy of the Nordic countries is generally small, open, and some with individual currency. They have to rely on other markets for growth and expansion, at the same time become vulnerable to external impact. Therefore, proper positioning in the international markets is crucial to national sustainability. Countries described in this volume provided both failed and successful examples. Icelandic banks overexpanded in the international financial markets with heavy reliance on foreign currency to the extent that the government had no ability to bail them out when the international market money dried up.

On the other hand, the better than EU average economic growth of Finland and Sweden for the past two decades has been attributed to their more open and more dynamic policies for international integration. Their rapid developments in the financial systems impacted positively on their growth prospects (Jonung, 2010). Although these two countries were also caught in the Icelandic and Baltic financial troubles in this financial crisis, their domestic markets were relatively well protected from this crisis. All Finland, Iceland, and Sweden have adopted the expansion strategy, yet the results are different after two decades. Therefore, national positioning in the international markets is an important lesson to be learned in retrospect.

Third, government's timely and strong leadership is critical for restoring public confidence when financial crisis unfolds. One of the key reasons for the relatively speedy recovery of Nordic countries (except Iceland) is the government's timely and strong intervention. Such measure was taken from the experience they learned after the early 1990s Nordic banking crisis. The lesson was that rapid, transparent, and determined government actions to maintain public confidence in national banking system reduced the impact of a financial crisis and allowed for a rapid recovery of the financial system and the real economy (Jonung, 2010). Research reveals that the reduced consumption often stems from psychological reasons rather than lower household income (Nanto, 2009). In other words, the decreasing public confidence often accelerates recession and commercial activities gradually stall. In this crisis, central banks of main Nordic countries have been accredited with their timely and proper intervening measures to stabilize the financial order. Even Sweden, often viewed as having a successful model, had to take decisive action to deal with the nonperforming assets of its banking system (Nanto).

Fourth, adopting smart and value creating investments in economic downturn will further enhance national well-being. Several Nordic countries have adopted smart investments in planning their stimulus packages. The old saying that "a crisis is also an opportunity" is very true. During this financial crisis, political unity was easier to achieve, as evidenced in Sweden; consensus of budget allocation was processed faster, evidenced by the fast streaming of annual budget into the stimulus package in the Nordic countries; and the key funding targets were easier to identify, evidenced by Nordic countries' quick focus on education, training, and green energy-efficient technology.

Generally speaking, Nordic countries are already very advanced in economic development. Their future threat is their aging populations and related reduced productivity, health-care, and pension problems. Taking the opportunity of resources reallocation in this financial crisis to invest in R&D, aging friendly and future-oriented technology may be a turning point to create a sustainable economy for the shrinking and gradually resource depleting societies.

Fifth, straightening the aftermath exit transition is essential to continuously benefit from the extra resources allocated through stimulus package during the financial crisis. During the crisis, most of the governments announced the stimulus package in relatively haste. Even though the package was well planned, oftentimes problems surfaced during the implementation stage. As some stimulus resources were streamed into multiyear projects, it is essential to reexamine the process and to evaluate the performance of each project in order to maximize the benefits of these extra resources. Some projects may need to be merged into routine practices, some need to be refocused, and some need to be discontinued altogether. In addition, structural barriers that hampered national development identified during the crisis need to be revisited for more deep-rooted reforms. Some stimulus also needs to be gradually phased out rather than a sudden stop in order not to disrupt the reviving economy. All relevant issues have to be displayed for open discussion to map out the aftermath strategies. Furthermore, continuous dialogue among relevant parties will bring national strengths as well as weakness to light in systems for better future crisis management.

Sixth, establishing a network of international alliance for mutual support may reduce future risks. One of the key factors enabling Iceland to walk out from its 2008 misery was the support of several countries (described in the section on Iceland in Chap. 4), other than IMF's assistance. In this increasingly deepening global economy, no nation can insulate itself from the outside world. For smaller economies like the Nordic countries, establishing a network of international alliance for mutual support is a measure to reinforce each other's competitiveness in the keen global competition. Practices like the currency swap facilities adopted by many countries in this financial crisis and Norway's reaching out to assist other countries in trouble are good examples of forming strategic international alliances. Yet, the precondition for successful functioning of such a network is to revise and strengthen international regulation and framework conditions for sound financial activities (Kredittilsynet, 2009).

Seventh, dynamically balancing various pulling forces may create a better environment and NIC ecosystem for future national development. From this financial disaster of Iceland, it is apparent that the banks' micromanagement was overpowered and squeezed the spaces of the government's macromanagement. Iceland's money market weight is skewed toward the foreign currency with a minor percentage of local currency, and the banks' heavy reliance on wholesale market funding rather than deposits in their balance sheets is an example of different pulling forces. In addition, the balance between regulation with surveillance control and respect for institution's autonomy is also a hard lesson. Therefore, dynamically striking a balance between various pulling forces needs to be grounded on continuously refined and effective governance systems that enable automatic scouting and correction for the best benefits of a nation.

Eighth, relying on a single source for national development is too risky for future sustainability. Several countries in this cluster have developed heavy reliance on one single source for national development. For example, Nokia has become an attractor in Finland, 40 % of Iceland's GDP relies on its fishing industry, and the petroleum revenue has a 30 % share of GDP in Norway. Although diversification has been given attention (such as Iceland's biotechnology), an accelerated pace may be required through the encouragement of entrepreneurship, setting up matching policies, and the collaboration between the knowledge triangle – government, universities, and industries.

Ninth, enhancing the added value of national intellectual capital may help sustain the Nordic countries. The World Economic Forum reports that Nordic countries are high in global competitiveness, so does our report that they are the top tier national intellectual capital (NIC) countries. What else can they do, since they are already at the top? Our research discloses a gap between their NIC and GDP growth. In other words, their advancement in NIC did not correlate with significant GDP growth. Therefore, the added value of their NIC can be enhanced for a more sustainable future. In addition, regular reviews of their internal advancement and external NIC competitiveness can also be conducted. Our research revealed that decreases in capital scores sometimes result in capital ranking increases, as in the case of Finland and Norway. The ranking gain is an external comparison with 48 countries and might be temporarily caused by other countries badly hurt by the global downturn, whereas a score decrease is more indicative of an internal decline. Therefore, ranking increase is not necessarily a positive sign; it has to be examined together with a score increase or decrease for better national intangible assets.

Tenth, attending to NIC development pattern over time through societal intelligence helps point out a better navigation direction for coping measures. In our research, Norway's development path is always distinctive from other countries, high in GDP yet relatively low in NIC. The decision makers in Norway are fully aware that their oil resources may deplete one day, which is the very reason they set up the global fund to benefit their future generations. Yet, it is also well recognized that the intangibles will be a key determinant of future competitiveness. Without good intellectual capital to carefully preserve or generate everlasting advantages, the tangibles will be consumed sooner or later. Therefore, attending to better NIC development should benefit Norway's future sustainability. A close model for Norway is Sweden. Sweden was number two in both human capital and renewal capital among the 48 countries (Table 3.1). After the financial crisis, its relatively weaker market capital and process capital not only had score increases but also showed ranking gains. That is, their four capitals (human, market, process, and renewal capital) are all at high levels, which resulted in their ranking number one in the 6 years NIC (Table 3.1).

Other development patterns that deserve attention include Denmark losing its process capital competitiveness after the financial crisis and Finland having comparatively low human capital even though its students' PISA performance is among the best in the whole world. Each country has its own characteristics and resources and may have different national development priorities, yet these signals deserve attention since the intangibles are carrying an increasingly important role in national well-being.

Concluding Remarks and Emerging Insights

This global financial crisis was triggered in September 2008 by US subprime mortgage problems. As a result, a massive impact on the world economy occurred with global financial conditions worsening, due to the drying up of the interbank market, combined with tougher lending terms, higher borrowing costs for companies, and tumbling stock markets. GDP shrunk worldwide as business and consumer confidence dropped, leading to a marked decline in corporate investments, major destocking, and a contraction in world trade, which was followed by a sharp deterioration in labor markets.

In the wake of the 2008 global financial crisis, it became clear that the crisis had its origin in the weak financial system, weak regulatory framework, and overexpanded debt-financed consumption. Although this global financial crisis came with unexpected speed and negative effects, the governments of these Nordic countries (except Iceland) navigated through the crisis relatively well, mainly because of their strengthened financial systems after the 1990s Nordic crisis. Crises entail opportunities as well. The 2008 global financial crisis has provided an excellent opportunity for nations to assess the policy responses, to uncover the structural flaws, to discuss the options for restoring economic growth, and to reconstruct a cleaner and more resilient economy.

Presumably, national leaders will have learned some valuable lessons from this financial crisis and will have better foresight to prevent similar crisis from happening again. However, such confidence comes from continuously responding to the social changes and reexamining the adequacy of national strategies, policies, and governance in coping with the increasingly interconnected and rapidly changing global economic environment. For the advanced economies like Nordic countries, future sustainability relies more on the intangibles such as NIC and societal innovation than the tangibles.

The growing importance of the intangibles has been testified by the US Bureau of Economic Analysis, which announced that effectively from July 2013, R&D will no longer be treated as a mere expense; it will be categorized on the government's books as an investment (Coy, 2013). Original works of art such as films, music, and books will also be regarded for the first time as long-lived assets. The NIC model introduced in this booklet series assists policy makers to find the position of their nations in the 48-country landscape and navigate future direction for effective resources allocation. Different from the rating agencies that rate national debt, NIC rates national capabilities for building a sustainable future. With the increase of Internet-connected knowledge and aging economies, our next model – sustainable national intellectual capital (SNIC) – will specifically emphasize the intangibles that facilitate national well-being in terms of friendly health-care system, easy connectivity and contactivity, effective educational system, sound government structure, and ongoing renewal system.

As a recap, to counter worsening economic conditions worldwide during the financial crisis (2008–2009), a total of US$2 trillion in stimulus packages, amounting to approximately 3 % of world gross domestic product, were allocated (some of the packages include measures that extend into subsequent years), an amount that exceeded the call by the International Monetary Fund for fiscal stimulus totaling 2 % of global GDP (Nanto, 2009).

This booklet briefly reports the main causes of why these five Nordic countries were dragged into the financial turmoil, how they came out of it, their positioning in the global NIC landscape, the NIC strength or weakness of each country, and the co-development of NIC and GDP. As concerns over the aging population, shrinking workforce, and reduced productivity become more and more pressing in these countries (except Iceland), the stimulus packages implemented during this financial crisis should bring some positive effects in rethinking these countries' future development. To fully benefit from each governments' extra resources inputs, the challenges and policy implications presented above provide some clues for building even more resilient economies for their future sustainability.

The global economic outlook in 2013 is promising (IMF, 2013). Major policy decisions have laid the foundations for a strengthening in confidence, and acute crisis risk has been reduced in the Euro area and the USA. However, Nordic countries were projected to have stagnated economies, except Sweden, in 2013 (Nordea, 2013). With the global economy picking up, 2014 was predicted to have a better prospect than 2013.

At the completion of reporting the impact of the financial crisis on these five Nordic countries from national intellectual capital perspective, we have a strong understanding that national success is an ability that accumulates over time meticulously; it does not come quickly nor at will. National economic development is built upon well-coordinated tangible and intangible systems, including money, real assets, and human capital, market capital, process capital, and renewal capital systems described in this booklet. As the very origin of the financial crisis is people, systems, governance, market dynamics, and global interdependence, they are also the keys to the economic recovery and national development in any country.

Appendices

Appendix 1: Summary of the Main Stimulus Packages of the Five Nordic Countries

Country	Date	Amount	Item
Denmark	Early Oct. 2008	#1 Bank Rescue Package I US$12.6bn (DKK70bn)	Bank Rescue Package I – a guarantee for all deposits with and loans to Danish banks. Nonresidents withdrew krone deposits totaling US$12.6bn (DKK70bn) from Danish banks
	Oct. 10, 2008 Jan. 18, 2009	#2 Bank Rescue Package II US $17.8bn (DKK100bn)	Financial stability to guarantee all deposits in Danish banks not covered by other means Bank Rescue Package II to ensure normal lending activity by banks Infusing a hybrid capital totaling US$17.8bn (DKK100bn) to Danish banks and mortgage banks and prolonging the government guarantee scheme on deposits to 2013

(continued)

C.Y.-Y. Lin et al., *National Intellectual Capital and the Financial Crisis in Denmark, Finland, Iceland, Norway, and Sweden*, SpringerBriefs in Economics,
DOI 10.1007/978-1-4614-9536-9, © The Author(s) 2014

Country	Date	Amount	Item
	Early 2009	#3 US$8,668mn mostly focused on bank aid and financial measures	Tax cuts, a major tax reform was legislated Release of funds from Special Pension scheme has significantly eased households' liquidity constraints
	2008–2010	#4 Fiscal packages US $8,668mn, stimulus package as 0.8 % of 2008 GDP	
Finland		#5 US$8,575mn	Aimed at the infrastructure (transport construction and broadband); energy and mining sectors; education, research, and training; and others as part of the Finnish Innovation Strategy
	May 2009	#4 1. US$1,231.2mn (€910mn, 0.48 % of 2008 GDP) 2. US$33.8mn (€25mn, 0.01 % of 2008 GDP) 3. US$40.6mn (€30mn, 0.02 % of 2008 GDP) 4. US$51.4mn (€38mn, 0.02 % of 2008 GDP)	1. Infrastructure 2. Science, R&D, and innovation 3. Education 4. Green technology
	2008–2010	#4, #6 Fiscal packages US $8,575mn, stimulus package as 0.3 % of 2008 GDP, 1.8 % of GDP in 2009, and 1.6 % of GDP in 2010	40 % of the measures represented tax cuts and the abolition of employers' national insurance contributions Approximately 20 % were categorized as "construction and renovation" and "civil engineering" About 2 % went to labor policy and education; about 3 % went to benefit increases

(continued)

Country	Date	Amount	Item
Iceland	Oct. 24, 2008	#8 US$2.1bn package was announced by IMF	Under IMF's fast-track emergency financing mechanism
	Nov. 19, 2008	US$827mn immediately available	IMF approved the 2-year Stand-By Arrangement for Iceland, making US $827mn immediately available and the remainder to be paid in eight equal installments, subject to quarterly reviews. IMF loan will fill about 42 % of the country's 2008–2010 financing gap. The remainder will be met by official bilateral creditors
	2008–2010	#4 Stimulus package – 1.7 % of 2008 GDP	
Norway	Oct. 12, 2008	#2	Norwegian government gave banks better access to liquidity and financing to calm and provide confidence in the financial market. New government paper with a limit of US$55.4bn (NOK350bn) gave banks access to collateral that could facilitate new long-term borrowing
			Norges Bank issues fixed rate loans (F-loans) with maturities of 2 and 3 years for smaller banks, removing the requirement of a minimum outstanding volume of US$47.5mn (NOK300mn) for securities issued in Norwegian kroner

(continued)

Country	Date	Amount	Item
		#9, #10 US$20.8bn (NOK 130bn) 3 % of GDP for Mainland Norway	Tax relief and measures for employment, welfare, and the environment. Emphasis on municipalities (schools, nursing homes, churches); construction (in particular transport and buildings with energy efficiency in mind); employment, readjustment, and skills; business R&D (direct grants and grants for Ph. D. students); ICTs (infrastructure, digitizing of government services, electronic signature, etc.); and green measures
	Feb. 2009	#11	US$2.38bn (NOK16.6bn) – extra budget spending
		US$2.87bn (NOK 20bn)	US$0.47bn (NOK3.3bn) – tax relief
	May 2009	#4	1. Infrastructure
		1. US$0.6bn (NOK3.8bn, 0.16 % of 2008 GDP)	
		2. US$26mn (NOK170mn, 0.01 % of 2008 GDP)	2. Science, R&D, and innovation
		3. US$41.3mn (NOK270mn, 0.01 % of 2008 GDP)	3. Education
		4. US$0.2bn (NOK1.6bn, 0.06 % of 2008 GDP)	4. Green technology
	2008–2009	#4 Stimulus package – 0.3 % of 2008 GDP	
	2009–2010	#7 Stimulus package – 0.8 % of 2008 GDP	

(continued)

Country	Date	Amount	Item
Sweden	Oct. 29, 2008	#2 #5	A guarantee program of up to US$195.2bn (SEK1500bn) to support banks' and building societies' medium-term financing A stability fund of US$2bn (SEK15bn) was set up to help future solvency problems at Swedish financial institutions
	Dec. 5, 2008	Fiscal policy – US$977.7mn (SEK8.3bn)	A fiscal policy package worth US$977.7mn (SEK8.3bn), equivalent to 1.3 % of GDP
	Dec. 11, 2008	US$3.5bn (SEK28bn)	A rescue package for the car industry worth US$3.5bn (SEK28bn)
	Oct. 2008	#10 US$482bn (SEK3,539bn)	Total US$482bn (SEK3,539bn) The government estimates the magnitude of the tax reductions and spending increases to total approximately US $11.3bn (SEK83bn), or approximately 2.7 % of GDP
	May 2009	#4 1. US$1.1bn (SEK8.6bn, 0.27 % of 2008 GDP) 2. US$1.1bn (SEK9bn, 0.29 % of 2008 GDP) 3. US$63.5mn (SEK500mn, 0.016 % of 2008 GDP) 4. US$0.3bn (SEK2bn, 0.06 % of 2008 GDP)	
	2008–2010	#4 Fiscal packages US $13,109mn, Stimulus packages – 0.3 % of 2008 GDP	

(continued)

Country	Date	Amount	Item
	2009–2010	#7	
		Stimulus program – 3.3 % of 2008 GDP	

1. Bernstein, N. (2010, March 22). Nils Bernstein: The Danish krone during the crisis. Speech by Mr. Nils Bernstein, Governor of the National Bank of Denmark, at the Copenhagen Business School, Copenhagen.
2. Kredittilsynet (2009, February). *The financial market in Norway 2008: Risk outlook.* Retrieved from http://www.finanstilsynet.no/Global/English/Reports/Risk%20Outlook%20Reports/Risk%20Outlook%202008.pdf
3. OECD (2009a). *OECD economic surveys: Denmark.* OECD Publishing
4. OECD (2009b, June). *Policy responses to the economic crisis: Investing in innovation for long-term growth.* Retrieved from http://www.oecd.org/dataoecd/59/45/42983414.pdf
5. OECD (2009c, May 11). Policy responses to the economic crisis: Stimulus packages, innovation and long-term growth. *Organisation for Economic Co-operation and Development*, DSTI/IND/STP/ICCP(2009)1/ADD/FINAL. Retrieved from http://www.oecd.org/officialdocuments/publicdisplaydocumentpdf/?cote=DSTI/IND/STP/ICCP(2009)1/ADD/FINAL&docLanguage=En
6. Lindvall, J. (2011). *Politics and policies in two economic crises.* Retrieved from http://www.tcd.ie/iiis/assets/pdf/Workshop25-26Feb2011-Lindvahl_Responding_to_the_Crisis[1].pdf
7. Breuss, F., Kaniovski, S., & Schratzenstaller, M. (2009). Macro-economic effects of the fiscal stimulus measures in Austria. *Austrian Economic Quarterly* (14.4), 205–216. Retrieved from http://fritz.breuss.wifo.ac.at/Breuss_Kaniovski_Schratzenstaller_Macro-economic_Effects_Fiscal_Stimulus_Austria_AEQ_4_2009.PDF
8. Andersen, C. (2008, December 8). Iceland gets help to recover from historic crisis. *International Monetary Fund (IMF).* Retrieved from http://www.imf.org/external/pubs/ft/survey/so/2008/int111908a.htm
9. Halvorsen, K. (2009, October 6). Norway less affected by the financial crises than many other countries. *Scan Magazine*. Retrieved from http://www.scanmagazine.co.uk/2009/10/norway-less-affected-by-the-financial-crises-than-many-other-countries/
10. Jochem, S. (2010). Sweden country report. In Bertelsmann Stiftung (Ed.), *Managing the crisis. A comparative assessment of economic governance in 14 economies.* Gütersloh: Bertelsmann Stiftung.
11. Reuters (2009, March 17). *FACTBOX-Europe's fiscal stimulus plans.* Retrieved from http://in.reuters.com/article/2009/03/17/eu-summit-stimulus-idINLH44404720090317

Appendix 2: Important Meetings Held by World Leaders to Address the 2008 Global Financial Crisis

Date	Place	Participants
June 18–19, 2012	Los Cabos, Mexico	G20
June 17, 2012	Los Cabos, Mexico	G7 finance ministers
March 1–2, 2012	Brussels	European Council
January 30, 2012	Brussels	Informal meeting of members of the European Council
December 8–9, 2011	Brussels	European Council
November 12–13, 2011	Honolulu, USA	19th APEC Economic Leaders' Meeting
November 3–4, 2011	Cannes, France	G20
October 23, 2011	Brussels	European Council
September 10, 2011	Marseille	G8 Deauville Partnership finance ministers
September 9–10, 2011	Marseille	G7 finance ministers and central bank governors
July 21, 2011	Brussels	Meeting of heads of state or government of the Euro area
June 23–24, 2011	Brussels	European Council
March 24–25, 2011	Brussels	European Council
March 17, 2011	Japan	G7 finance ministers telephone conference
March 11, 2011	Brussels	Extraordinary European Council
February 4, 2011	Brussels	European Council
December 16–17, 2010	Brussels	European Council
November 21, 2010	Ireland	G7 finance ministers
November 13–14, 2010	Yokohama, Japan	18th APEC Economic Leaders' Meeting
November 11–12, 2010	Seoul, Korea	G20
October 28–29, 2010	Brussels	European Council
October 8, 2010	Washington DC	G7 finance ministers and central bank governors
September 16, 2010	Brussels	European Council
June 26–27, 2010	Toronto, Canada	G20
June 17, 2010	Brussels	European Council
March 25–26, 2010	Brussels	European Council
February 11, 2010	Brussels	Informal meeting of heads of state or government of the European Union
February 5–6, 2010	Iqaluit, Nunavut, Canada	G7 finance ministers and central bank governors
December 10–11, 2009	Brussels	European Council
November 19, 2009	Brussels	Informal meeting of heads of state or government of the European Union
November 14–15, 2009	Singapore	17th APEC Economic Leaders' Meeting

(continued)

Date	Place	Participants
October 29–30, 2009	Brussels	European Council
October 3, 2009	Istanbul, Turkey	G7 finance ministers and central bank governors
September 24–25, 2009	Pittsburgh, USA	G20
September 17, 2009	Brussels	Informal meeting of heads of state or government of the European Union
June 18–19, 2009	Brussels	European Council
June 12–13, 2009	Lecce, Italy	G8 finance ministers
April 24, 2009	Washington, D.C.	G7 finance ministers and central bank governors
April 2, 2009	G20 London Summit, UK	G20
March 19–20, 2009	Brussels	European Council
February 2009	Rome	G7 finance ministers and central bank governors
December 11–12, 2008	Brussels	European Council
November 2008	Peru	G20 APEC
November 22–23, 2008	Lima, Peru	16th APEC Economic Leaders' Meeting
November 14–15, 2008	Washington, D.C., USA	G7
October 15–16, 2008	Brussels	European Council
October 10, 2008	Washington, D.C.	G7 finance ministers
September 1, 2008	Brussels	Extraordinary European Council
July 7–9, 2008	Tokyo, Japan	34th G8 Summit
June 19–20, 2008	Brussels	European Council
June 13–14, 2008	Osaka	G8 finance ministers' meeting
March 13–14, 2008	Brussels	European Council
February 9, 2008	Tokyo	G7 finance ministers' and central bank governors' meeting

For further information:
http://g20mexico.org/en/g20/previous-leaders-summits
http://www.g8.utoronto.ca/finance/index.htm
http://video.consilium.europa.eu/ecofin/
http://www.european-council.europa.eu/council-meetings/conclusions
http://www.apec.org/

Appendix 3: Indicators in Each Type of Capital

Human capital index	**Market capital index**
1. Skilled labor*	1. Corporate tax*
2. Employee training*	2. Cross-border venture*
3. Literacy rate	3. Openness of culture*
4. Higher education enrollment	4. Globalization*
5. Pupil–teacher ratio	5. Transparency*
6. Internet subscribers	6. Image of country*
7. Public expenditure on education	7. Exports of goods
Process capital index	**Renewal capital index**
1. Business competition environment*	1. Business R&D spending
2. Government efficiency*	2. Basic research*
3. Intellectual property rights protection*	3. R&D spending/GDP
4. Capital availability*	4. R&D researchers
5. Computers in use per capita	5. Cooperation between universities and enterprises*
6. Convenience of establishing new firms*	6. Scientific articles
7. Mobile phone subscribers	7. Patents per capita (USPTO + EPO)

Remarks:

1. Financial capital is the logarithm of GDP per capita adjusted by purchasing power parity
2. Indicators marked with an asterisk (*) are rated qualitatively using a scale of 1–10
3. Indicators with objective numbers are transformed to 1–10 scores, by calculating the ratio to the highest number in that indicator and then multiply 10
4. Readers can refer to the book *National Intellectual Capital: A Comparison of 40 Countries* for model validation details (www.nic40.org)

Appendix 4: Definition of the 29 Indicators

Indicators	Definition
Human capital	
Skilled labor*	Whether skilled labor is readily available
Employee training*	Whether employee training is a high propriety in companies
Literacy rate	Adult (over 15 years) literacy rate as a percentage of population
Higher education enrollment	Percentage of population that has attained at least tertiary education
Pupil–teacher ratio	Ratio of teaching staff to students
Internet subscribers	Number of internet users per 1,000 people
Public expenditure on education	Total public expenditure on education (percentage of GDP)
Market capital	
Corporate tax encouragement*	Whether corporate taxes encourage entrepreneurial activity
Cross-border venture*	Whether international transactions can be freely negotiated with foreign partners
Openness to foreign culture*	Whether the national culture is open to foreign culture ideas
Attitudes toward globalization*	Whether attitudes toward globalization are generally positive in a given society
Transparency*	Whether transparency of government policy is satisfactory
Country image*	Whether the image abroad of a given country encourages business development
Exports of goods	Exports of goods (percentage of GDP)
Process capital	
Business competition environment*	Whether competition legislation is efficient in preventing unfair competition
Government efficiency*	Whether government bureaucracy hinders business activity
Intellectual property rights protection*	Whether intellectual property rights are adequately enforced
Capital availability*	Whether cost of capital encourages business development
Computers in use per capita	Number of computers per 1,000 people
Convenience of establishing new firms*	Whether creation of firms is supported by legislation
Mobile phone subscribers	Number of subscribers per 1,000 inhabitants
Renewal capital	
Business R&D spending	Business expenditure on R&D (per capita)
Basic research*	Whether basic research enhances long-term economic development
R&D spending/GDP	Total expenditure on R&D (percentage of GDP)
R&D researchers	Total R&D personnel nationwide per capita (full-time work equivalent per 1,000 people)
Cooperation between universities and enterprises*	Whether knowledge transfer is highly developed between universities and companies
Scientific articles	Scientific articles published by origin of author (per capita)
Patents per capita (USPTO + EPO)	USPTO and EPO total patents granted (per capita)
Financial capital	
GDP per capita (PPP) (from IMF)	Gross domestic product based on purchasing power parity (PPP) per capita

Appendix 5: 48 Countries by Cluster and by Continent

This booklet series covers a total of 48 countries in 11 country clusters. China, Brazil, and South Africa are grouped twice to maintain cluster completeness. China is in both Greater China region and BRICKS region, Brazil is in both BRICKS region and Latin American region, and South Africa is in both BRICKS region and in Cluster 5.

Eleven country clusters:

1. Portugal, Italy, Greece, Spain
2. Greater China region (China, Hong Kong, Singapore, Taiwan)
3. Brazil, Russia, India, China, Korea, South Africa (BRICKS)
4. Indonesia, Malaysia, the Philippines, Thailand
5. Israel, Jordan, Turkey, South Africa
6. Bulgaria, Czech Republic, Hungary, Romania, Poland
7. Austria, Belgium, the Netherlands, Switzerland
8. France, Germany, Ireland, the UK
9. Argentina, Brazil, Chile, Colombia, Mexico, Venezuela
10. Australia, Canada, Japan, New Zealand, the USA
11. Denmark, Finland, Iceland, Norway, Sweden

Forty-eight countries by continent:

Europe – 24 countries

Nordic Europe – Denmark, Finland, Iceland, Norway, and Sweden

Western Europe – Austria, Belgium, France, Germany, Ireland, Netherlands, Switzerland, and the UK

Southern Europe – Greece, Italy, Portugal, and Spain

Eastern Europe – Russia

East Central Europe – Bulgaria, Czech Republic, Hungary, Poland, Romania, and Turkey

Americas – eight countries
North America – Canada, the USA
Latin America – Argentina, Brazil, Chile, Colombia, Mexico, Venezuela

Australia – two countries
Australia, New Zealand

Asia – 13 countries
East Asia – China, Hong Kong, Japan, Korea, Taiwan
West Asia – Israel, Jordan
Southeast Asia – Indonesia, Malaysia, Philippines, Singapore, Thailand
South Asia – India

Africa – one country
South Africa

Appendix 6: National Intellectual Capital Scores and Ranking Comparison for 48 Countries (2005–2010)

2005–2010	Human capital		Market capital		Process capital		Renewal capital		Financial capital		Overall IC	
Mean	6.420		5.409		5.345		3.658		9.115		29.946	
SD	1.217		1.085		1.454		2.056		0.690		5.840	
Country	Score	Ranking	Score	Ranking	Score	Ranking	Score	Ranking	Score	Ranking	Score	Ranking
Argentina	5.370	36	3.340	47	3.038	47	1.413	45	8.755	34	21.916	45
Australia	7.205	15	6.199	12	6.938	9	4.927	16	9.695	11	34.964	13
Austria	7.229	14	6.203	11	6.982	8	5.296	12	9.708	10	35.418	11
Belgium/Lux	7.666	8	5.519	23	5.924	21	4.706	17	9.635	14	33.450	19
Brazil	4.757	44	4.589	38	3.076	46	1.753	36	8.481	40	22.656	42
Bulgaria	5.493	34	4.929	31	4.054	36	1.589	41	8.646	37	24.710	35
Canada	7.855	6	6.137	13	6.464	15	5.064	14	9.710	9	35.229	12
Chile	5.414	35	6.663	5	5.163	28	1.710	37	8.784	32	27.734	30
China	4.942	39	5.184	28	3.746	40	2.099	33	7.967	44	23.938	40
Columbia	4.941	40	4.677	36	3.951	37	1.435	44	8.348	42	23.352	41
Czech Republic	5.995	30	5.720	18	5.378	25	2.905	24	9.271	27	29.269	25
Denmark	**8.545**	**1**	**6.662**	**6**	**7.642**	**1**	**6.587**	**6**	**9.665**	**13**	**39.101**	**3**
Finland	**7.601**	**9**	**6.232**	**10**	**7.399**	**3**	**7.755**	**3**	**9.606**	**17**	**38.593**	**4**
France	6.956	20	4.141	45	5.730	22	4.500	20	9.585	18	30.912	23
Germany	6.761	23	5.630	19	6.489	14	5.796	9	9.612	16	34.287	17
Greece	5.986	31	4.216	43	4.113	35	2.168	32	9.440	23	25.923	31
Hong Kong	6.564	25	8.090	2	7.209	5	3.277	23	9.794	4	34.934	14
Hungary	6.674	24	4.836	32	5.095	29	2.301	29	9.046	29	27.952	29
Iceland	**8.357**	**3**	**5.614**	**21**	**6.561**	**12**	**5.931**	**8**	**9.713**	**8**	**36.154**	**8**
India	3.926	48	5.620	20	3.556	42	1.954	34	7.285	48	22.340	44
Indonesia	4.062	47	4.832	33	3.257	44	1.519	42	7.594	46	21.263	47
Ireland	7.145	16	6.816	3	6.711	11	4.101	21	9.768	5	34.541	16
Israel	8.040	4	5.954	16	6.454	17	7.091	4	9.414	24	36.953	6
Italy	6.471	28	4.155	44	5.184	27	2.745	26	9.479	22	28.035	28

(continued)

Appendix 6 (continued)

2005–2010	Human capital		Market capital		Process capital		Renewal capital		Financial capital		Overall IC	
Mean	6.420		5.409		5.345		3.658		9.115		29.946	
SD	1.217		1.085		1.454		2.056		0.690		5.840	
Country	Score	Ranking	Score	Ranking	Score	Ranking	Score	Ranking	Score	Ranking	Score	Ranking
Japan	7.581	10	4.820	34	6.209	18	6.473	7	9.576	19	34.659	15
Jordan	5.345	37	5.341	26	4.411	32	2.212	30	7.865	45	25.174	33
Korea	6.964	19	5.123	29	5.282	26	4.595	19	9.383	25	31.348	22
Malaysia	6.538	26	6.410	9	5.567	23	2.186	31	8.740	35	29.442	24
Mexico	4.871	42	4.491	39	3.226	45	1.237	48	8.781	33	22.606	43
Netherlands	7.312	12	6.761	4	6.879	10	5.163	13	9.739	7	35.855	10
New Zealand	7.123	18	5.999	15	6.460	16	3.701	22	9.380	26	32.662	21
Norway	**7.936**	**5**	**6.055**	**14**	**7.008**	**7**	**4.961**	**15**	**9.987**	**1**	**35.947**	**9**
Philippines	4.772	43	4.464	40	3.317	43	1.268	47	7.481	47	21.302	46
Poland	6.393	29	4.246	41	3.895	38	1.819	35	8.945	30	25.299	32
Portugal	6.882	22	4.801	35	5.470	24	2.467	27	9.224	28	28.844	26
Romania	5.829	32	4.219	42	3.806	39	1.685	38	8.594	39	24.133	39
Russia	5.530	33	3.860	46	3.588	41	2.349	28	8.822	31	24.150	38
Singapore	7.144	17	8.306	1	7.506	2	5.416	11	9.961	2	38.334	5
South Africa	4.708	45	4.976	30	4.472	31	1.677	39	8.472	41	24.306	37
Spain	6.524	27	4.649	37	5.033	30	2.787	25	9.484	21	28.476	27
Sweden	**8.385**	**2**	**6.563**	**7**	**7.174**	**6**	**7.780**	**2**	**9.673**	**12**	**39.575**	**1**
Switzerland	7.575	11	6.481	8	7.374	4	7.988	1	9.753	6	39.172	2
Taiwan	7.244	13	5.823	17	6.026	20	5.425	10	9.526	20	34.044	18
Thailand	5.310	38	5.524	22	4.365	33	1.436	43	8.304	43	24.938	34
Turkey	4.703	46	5.227	27	4.167	34	1.666	40	8.690	36	24.453	36
UK	6.939	21	5.440	24	6.090	19	4.697	18	9.626	15	32.793	20
USA	7.695	7	5.348	25	6.558	13	6.715	5	9.886	3	36.202	7
Venezuela	4.884	41	2.761	48	2.545	48	1.277	46	8.625	38	20.092	48

Appendix 7: Country Profile: Additional Statistics

1. International reserves in millions of US dollars

Country	2005	2006	2007	2008	2009	2010
Denmark	40,157	28,558	31,303	36,991	45,791	73,725
Finland	11,047	6,016	6,347	7,651	6,782	9,354
Iceland	955	1,093	2,312	2,817	3,088	3,746
Norway	43,110	45,313	56,956	55,597	46,579	53,593
Sweden	21,205	21,330	25,356	27,735	23,854	42,089

Source: Global Finance http://www.gfmag.com/

2. GDP per capita – PPP – current international dollar

Country	2005	2006	2007	2008	2009	2010
Denmark	33,528	35,689	37,187	37,376	35,523	36,450
Finland	30,436	32,680	35,278	36,205	33,382	34,585
Iceland	35,272	37,133	39,763	40,793	37,957	36,621
Norway	47,520	49,756	52,065	52,870	51,988	52,013
Sweden	33,146	35,532	37,513	37,800	35,805	38,031

Source: World Economic Outlook Database http://www.imf.org/external/ns/cs.aspx?id=28

3. GDP (PPP) – share of world total_%

Country	2005	2006	2007	2008	2009	2010
Denmark	0.32	0.32	0.30	0.29	0.28	0.27
Finland	0.28	0.28	0.28	0.28	0.26	0.25
Iceland	0.02	0.02	0.02	0.02	0.02	0.02
Norway	0.39	0.38	0.37	0.36	0.36	0.34
Sweden	0.53	0.52	0.51	0.50	0.48	0.48

Source: World Economic Outlook Database http://www.imf.org/external/ns/cs.aspx?id=28

4. *Gross domestic expenditure on R&D as a percent of GDP*

Country	2005	2006	2007	2008	2009	2010
Denmark	2.61	2.44	2.43	2.55	2.72	3.02
Finland	3.48	3.48	3.45	3.47	3.5	3.96
Iceland	2.87	2.83	–	–	2.65	2.64
Norway	1.73	1.48	1.48	1.57	1.62	1.8
Sweden	3.95	3.86	3.73	3.64	3.75	3.62

Source: IMD World Competitiveness Yearbook 2006–2011

5. *Household saving rates: percent of disposable household income*

Country	2005	2006	2007	2008	2009	2010
Denmark	−4.2	−2.3	−4.0	−3.3	−0.5	−1.7
Finland	0.9	−1.1	−0.9	0.0	4.5	4.3
Iceland						
Norway	10.1	0.1	1.5	3.7	7.3	7.4
Sweden	5.5	6.6	8.8	11.2	12.9	10.7

Source: Global Finance http://www.gfmag.com/

Glossary

BBC British Broadcasting Corporation
CBI Central Bank of Iceland
CIA The USA Central Intelligence Agency
CPI Consumer price inflation
ECB European Central Bank
EU European Union
EMU Economic and Monetary Union
FDI Foreign Direct Investment
FSA Financial Supervisory Authority
GBF Government Bond Fund in Norway
GCI GCI Global Competitiveness Index (published by World Economic Forum)
GDP Gross domestic product
GDP per capita (ppp) Gross domestic product per capita adjusted by purchasing power parity
GIEK The Norwegian Guarantee Institute for Export Credits
HC Human capital
ICT Information and communication technology
IMD International Institute for Management Development
IMF International Monetary Fund
Long-term NIC Long-term-oriented national intellectual capital, represented by human capital and renewal capital
MC Market capital
NIC National intellectual capital
NOK Norwegian currency
OECD Organization for Economic Cooperation and Development
PC Process capital
Ppp Purchasing power parity
R&D Research and development
RC Renewal capital
SBA Iceland's Stand-By Arrangement with IMF
SD Standard Deviation

C.Y.-Y. Lin et al., *National Intellectual Capital and the Financial Crisis in Denmark, Finland, Iceland, Norway, and Sweden*, SpringerBriefs in Economics, DOI 10.1007/978-1-4614-9536-9, © The Author(s) 2014

SEK Swedish currency

Short-term NIC Short-term-oriented national intellectual capital, represented by market capital and process capital

SMEs Small- and medium-sized enterprises

SNIC Sustainable national intellectual capital

Three time periods For the convenience of comparing ranking changes, the 6-year data were separated into three time periods, namely, 2005–2006, 2007–2008, and 2009–2010. Two years each represents "before, during, and after" the 2008 global financial crisis. Even though Euro zone is still in sovereign debt trouble as of mid-2012, the time partition is based on the financial crisis progression in the epicenter. The signs of financial trouble appeared in 2007 and the crisis was declared over in the third quarter of 2009.

USPTO The United States Patent and Trademark Office

References

BBC. (2008, October 10). Councils 'not reckless with cash'. *BBC*. Retrieved from http://news.bbc.co.uk/2/hi/uk_news/politics/7660438.stm

Bernstein, N. (2010). The Danish krone during the crisis. Speech by Mr. Nils Bernstein, Governor of the National Bank of Denmark at the Copenhagen Business School, March 22, 2010. Retrieved from http://www.bis.org/review/r100325c.pdf

Brogger, T., & Einarsdottir, H. K. (2008, November 20). Iceland gets $4.6 billion bailout from IMF, Nordics. *Bloomberg*. Retrieved from http://www.bloomberg.com/apps/news?pid=newsarchive&sid=a3Zf1f9IBUWg&refer=europe

Bryant, L. (2011, September 8). Growth expected to slow in world's largest economies. *Voice of America News*. Retrieved from http://www.voanews.com/english/news/europe/OECD–Economic-Slowdown-Likely-to-Continue-129458543.html

Carey, D. (2009). Iceland: The financial and economic crisis. *OECD Economics Department working paper No. 725*. Retrieved from http://www.oecd.org/officialdocuments/displaydocumentpdf/?cote=eco/wkp(2009)66&doclanguage=en

Carlsen, I., Hytti, H., Thorlacius, S., Sundell, T., Ellingsen, J., Kalsto, A. M., et al. (2011). *Youth unemployment in the Nordic countries: A study on the rights of and measures for young jobseekers, Nordic Social Statistical Committee*. Albertslund: Schultz Information. ISBN 978-87-90248-55-0. Also available on www.nom-nos.dk or http://nososco-eng.nom-nos.dk/filer/publikationer/Youth%20Unemployment.pdf

Carstensen, M. B. (2011). New financial regulation in Denmark after the crisis – or the politics of not really doing anything. In *Danish foreign policy yearbook 2011*. Retrieved from http://www.isn.ethz.ch/isn/Digital-Library/Publications/Detail/?ord588=grp1&ots591=0c54e3b3-1e9c-be1e-2c24-a6a8c7060233&lng=en&id=131585

Central Bank of Iceland (CBI). (2008, October 14). *The Central Bank of Iceland draws on swap facility arrangements*. Central Bank of Iceland. http://www.cb.is/publications-news-and-speeches/news-and-speeches/news/2008/10/14/The-Central-Bank-of-Iceland-draws-on-swap-facility-arrangements

Central Bank of Iceland (CBI). (2010, December). *Monetary policy in Iceland after capital controls: report from the Central Bank of Iceland to the Minister of Economic Affairs* (Rep. No. 4). Retrieved from http://www.cb.is/library/Skr%C3%A1arsafn—EN/Reports/Monetary%20policy%20in%20Iceland%20after%20capital%20controls.pdf

Central Intelligence Agency (CIA). (2011). *The World Factbook*, U.S.A. Central Intelligence Agency. Retrieved from https://www.cia.gov/library/publications/the-world-factbook/index.html

Coy, P. (2013, July 18). The rise of the intangible economy: U.S. GDP counts R&D, artistic creation. *Bloomberg Business Week*. Retrieved from http://www.businessweek.com/articles/2013-07-18/the-rise-of-the-intangible-economy-u-dot-s-dot-gdp-counts-r-and-d-artistic-creation

C.Y.-Y. Lin et al., *National Intellectual Capital and the Financial Crisis in Denmark, Finland, Iceland, Norway, and Sweden*, SpringerBriefs in Economics,
DOI 10.1007/978-1-4614-9536-9, © The Author(s) 2014

Dutch News. (2008, November 20). *Dutch €1.3bn loan to Iceland agreed*. Retrieved from http://www.dutchnews.nl/news/archives/2008/11/dutch_13bn_loan_to_iceland_agr.php

Economic Freedom. (2011). *The Heritage Foundation leadership for America*. Retrieved from http://www.heritage.org/

Edvinsson, L., & Malone, M. S. (1997). *Intellectual capital: Realizing your company's true value by finding its hidden brainpower*. New York: Harper Business.

Europa. (2008, November 26). *The Commission launches a major recovery plan for growth and jobs, to boost demand and restore confidence in the European economy*. Retrieved from http://europa.eu/rapid/pressReleasesAction.do?reference=IP/08/1771

European Union (EU). (2013) *Flexicurity, Employment, Social Affairs & Inclusion, European Commission*. Retrieved August 7, 2013, from http://ec.europa.eu/social/main.jsp?catId=102&langId=en

Ewing, J. (2009, October 7). The apprentice: Germany's answer to jobless youth. *Bloomberg Businessweek Magazine*. Retrieved from http://www.businessweek.com/magazine/content/09_42/b4151033735128.htm

Freden, J. (2008). *Soft landing for Sweden in financial crisis*. Sweden.se. Retrieved from http://www.sweden.se/eng/Home/Business/Economy/Reading/Soft-landing-for-Sweden-in-financial-crisis/

Gecodia.com. (2013, July 18). *Economic outlook Iceland, Economic research for investors*. Retrieved July 18, 2013, from http://www.gecodia.com/Economic-Outlook-Iceland_a1836.html

Global Finance. (2013a). Country report. Retrieved from http://www.gfmag.com/

Global Finance. (2013b). *World's GDP growth by region, Global Finance*. Retrieved July 15, 2013, from http://www.gfmag.com/component/content/article/119-economic-data/12376-economic-dataworlds-gdp-growth-by-regionhtml.html#axzz2Z8YBShkn

Gurria, A. (2011). Overview of the economic survey of Sweden 2011. *OECD*. Retrieved from http://www.oecd.org/document/34/0,3746,en_2649_33733_46897250_1_1_1_1,00.html

Halvorsen, K. (2009, October 6). Norway less affected by the financial crises than many other countries. *Scan Magazine*. Retrieved from http://www.scanmagazine.co.uk/2009/10/norway-less-affected-by-the-financial-crises-than-many-other-countries/

Hassler, J. (2010). *Sweden in past, current and future economic crises – a report for the OECD Economics Department*. Retrieved from http://hassler-j.iies.su.se/PAPERS/OECDSwedenAug2010.pdf

Heritage Foundation. (2012). *Economic freedom*. Retrieved from http://www.heritage.org

IceNews. (2009, February 4). *Finnish government releases huge stimulus package, IceNews: News from the Nordics*. Retrieved from http://www.icenews.is/2009/02/04/finnish-government-releases-huge-stimulus-package/

Ingves, S. (2002). The Nordic banking crisis from an international perspective. Speech by the Director of Monetary and Exchange Affairs Department, International Monetary Fund in Oslo, September 11, 2002. Retrieved from http://www.imf.org/external/np/speeches/2002/091102.htm

International Monetary Fund (IMF). (2012, January 24). *World economic outlook update: Global recovery stalls, downside risks intensify*. International Monetary Fund. Retrieved from http://www.imf.org/external/pubs/ft/weo/2012/update/01/

International Monetary Fund (IMF). (2013, April). *World economic outlook: Hopes, realities, and risks*. Chapter 1: Global prospects and policies. Retrieved July 14, 2013, from http://www.imf.org/external/pubs/ft/weo/2013/01/pdf/c1.pdf

IPEZone. (2012, March 1). *German apprenticeship vs. CUS/UK uni-jobless system, International Political Economy Zone*. Retrieved from http://www.businessweek.com/magazine/content/09_42/b4151033735128.htm

Jochem, S. (2010). Sweden country report. In S. Bertelsmann (Ed.), *Managing the crisis. A comparative assessment of economic governance in 14 economies*. Gütersloh: Bertelsmann Stiftung.

Jonung, L. (2010). *Lessons from the Nordic financial crisis*. Prepared for the American Economic Association Annual meeting, Denver January 6–9, 2011. Retrieved from http://www.aeaweb.org/aea/2011conference/program/preliminary.php

Juel, S. (2011). *How to rebuild confidence in markets? The Norwegian experience*. EFTA Conference on small European economies: Weathering the storm of the financial and economic crisis, Brussels, November 16, 2011. Retrieved from http://www.efta.int/~/media/Documents/advisory-bodies/joint-consultative-parliamentary/Presentation_-_Juel.pdf

Kehoe, T. (2010, February). *The current financial crisis in Spain: What should we learn from the great depressions of the twentieth century?* University of Minnesota and Federal Reserve Bank of Minneapolis, 18th Barcelona Lecture, Barcelona G.S.E. and Banc Sabadell.

Kennedy, S. (2008, October 16). ECB power grows beyond borders as neighbors seek aid. Bloomberg. Retrieved from http://www.bloomberg.com/apps/news?pid=newsarchive&sid=ahVJCzeiIPhs

Kredittilsynet. (2009, February). *The financial market in Norway 2008: Risk outlook*. Retrieved from http://www.finanstilsynet.no/Global/English/Reports/Risk%20Outlook%20Reports/Risk%20Outlook%202008.pdf

Lin, G. T. (2009). The characteristics of Finland economy. *Taiwan International Studies Quarterly, 5*(4), 25–48 (in Chinese).

Lin, C. Y. Y., & Edvinsson, L. (2011). *National intellectual capital: A comparison of 40 countries*. New York: Springer.

Lindvall, J. (2011). *Politics and policies in two economic crises*. Lund University. Retrieved from http://www.tcd.ie/iiis/assets/pdf/Workshop25-26Feb2011-Lindvahl_Responding_to_the_Crisis[1].pdf

Mason, R. (2008). UK Treasury lends Iceland £2.2bn to compensate Icesave customers. *The Telegraph*. Retrieved from http://www.telegraph.co.uk/finance/financialcrisis/3491442/UK-Treasury-lends-Iceland-2.2bn-to-compensate-Icesave-customers.html

Mendonça, J. R. (2010). *The impact of the international financial crisis on Brazil*. Retrieved from http://www.realinstitutoelcano.org/wps/portal/rielcano_eng/Content?WCM_GLOBAL_CONTEXT=/elcano/elcano_in/zonas_in/international+economy/ari38-2010

Nanto, D. K. (2009). The global financial crisis: Analysis and policy implications. *CRS Report for Congress, Congressional Research Service 7–5700, RL34742*, October 2, 2009.

Nordea. (2013, June). *Economic outlook Nordics: Out of breeze, Nordea*. Retrieved July 18, 2013, from http://research.nordeamarkets.com/en/files/NU-EN-06-2013.pdf

Norwegian Confederation of Trade Union. (2010, February). *Some basic facts about the Norwegian economy*. Department of Economic and Social Affairs, Norwegian Confederation of Trade Union. Retrieved from http://www.lo.no/Documents/samfunn/2010_February.pdf

Oberg, S. (2009). *Sweden and the financial crisis*. Speech by the Deputy Governor of the Sveriges Riksbank at Carlson Investment Management, Stockholm, 20 January 2009. Retrieved from http://www.bis.org/review/r090128d.pdf?frames=0

OECD. (2009, November 5). *Economic survey of Denmark 2009: Denmark: The crisis and beyond*. Retrieved from http://www.oecd.org/document/23/0,3746,en_33873108_33873309_43964951_1_1_1_1,00.html

OECD. (2010, April 7). *Economic survey of Finland 2010: Overcoming the crisis and beyond*. Retrieved from http://www.oecd.org/document/45/0,3746,en_2649_33733_44900461_1_1_1_1,00.html

OECD. (2011a). *Government at a glance 2011, Country note: Finland*. Retrieved from http://www.oecd.org/dataoecd/60/25/47876433.pdf

OECD. (2011b, June). *Economic surveys of Iceland 2011*. Retrieved from http://www.oecd.org/document/16/0,3746,en_2649_33733_43946384_1_1_1_1,00.html

OECD. (2013). Iceland. In *OECD Economic Outlook, Vol. 2013 Issue 1*. OECD Publishing. doi:10.1787/eco_outlook-v2013-1-21-en#_blank#10.1787/eco_outlook-v2013-1-21-en

Oquist, G., & Benner, M. (2012, December). *Fostering breakthrough research: A comparative study*. The Royal Swedish Academy of Sciences. Retrieved August 5, 2013, from http://kva.se/Documents/Vetenskap_samhallet/Forskningspolitik/2012/akademirapport_breakthrough_research_121209.pdf

Palkamo, A. (2011, August 9). *WEF ranks Finland as the fourth most competitive nation*. Tekes. Retrieved from http://www.tekes.fi/en/community/News/482/News/1344?name=WEF+ranks+Finland+as+the+fourth+most+competitive+nation

Phillips, B. (2011, December 16). *Does Iceland want to join the EU? Aljazeera*. Retrieved from http://blogs.aljazeera.net/europe/2011/12/16/does-iceland-want-join-eu

Powell, N. (2011, October 26). How Finland's economy became hooked on Nokia. *The Globe and Mail*. Retrieved from http://www.theglobeandmail.com/report-on-business/economy/economy-lab/daily-mix/how-finlands-economy-became-hooked-on-nokia/article2214216/

RBA (Reserve Bank of Australia). (2012, August). Overview: Australia. Retrieved from http://www.rba.gov.au/publications/smp/2012/aug/pdf/overview.pdf

Reavis, C. (2009, July 22). The global financial crisis of 2008–2009: The role of greed, fear and oligarchs. *MIT Sloan Management Case #09-093*.

Reinhart, C. M., & Rogoff, K. S. (2009). *This time is different: Eight centuries of financial folly*. Princeton: Princeton University Press. ISBN 9780691142166.

RTE News. (2011, September 16). *Danish Prime Minister concedes defeat*. Retrieved from http://www.rte.ie/news/2011/0915/denmark.html

Schwab, K. (Ed.). (2011). *The global competitiveness report 2011–2012*. Geneva: World Economic Forum.

Stjernlöf, P. (2013, June 10). *Swedish top-tier research in need of reinforcement*. The Royal Swedish Academy of Science Press Release. Retrieved July 31, 2013, from http://www.kva.se/en/pressroom/Press-releases-2013/Swedish-top-tier-research-in-need-of-reinforcement/

Tervanen, K. (2009, May 29). Impact of financial crisis on the banking sector. *International Law Office*. Retrieved from http://www.internationallawoffice.com/newsletters/detail.aspx?g=f31ced90-bf62-48e9-8004-19069e83f5eb

The Mortgage Professor. (2009, September 21). *The mortgage crisis: US versus Denmark*. Retrieved from http://www.mtgprofessor.com/A%20-%20Type%20of%20Loan%20Provider/The%20Mortgage%20Crisis%20in%20US%20Versus%20Denmark.html

Valdimarsson, O. (2009, August 28). Iceland parliament approved debt bill. *Reuters*. Retrieved from http://www.reuters.com/article/2009/08/28/businesspro-us-iceland-debts-idUSTRE57R3B920090828

Ward, A. (2011, June 8). Iceland to raise $1B in bond sale. *Financial Times*. Retrieved from http://www.ft.com/intl/cms/s/264b7972-91fc-11e0-b8c1-00144feab49a,Authorised=false.html?_i_location=http%3A%2F%2Fwww.ft.com%2Fcms%2Fs%2F0%2F264b7972-91fc-11e0-b8c1-00144feab49a.html&_i_referer=http%3A%2F%2Fwww.institutionalinvestor.com%2FArticle%2F2845172%2FIceland-To-Raise-1B-In-Bond-Sale.html%3FArticleId%3D2845172#axzz1OYFDsGIv

World Bank (2012, January 18) Global economic prospects 2012a: Uncertainties and Vulnerabilities, World Bank Prospects. Retrieved from http://econ.worldbank.org/WBSITE/EXTERNAL/EXTDEC/EXTDECPROSPECTS/0,,contentMDK:23064688~pagePK:64165401~piPK:64165026~theSitePK:476883,00.html

Author Index

C.Y.-Y. Lin et al., *National Intellectual Capital and the Financial Crisis in Denmark, Finland, Iceland, Norway, and Sweden*, SpringerBriefs in Economics,
DOI 10.1007/978-1-4614-9536-9,

Subject Index

C.Y.-Y. Lin et al., *National Intellectual Capital and the Financial Crisis in Denmark, Finland, Iceland, Norway, and Sweden*, SpringerBriefs in Economics,
DOI 10.1007/978-1-4614-9536-9,

MIX
Papier aus verantwortungsvollen Quellen
Paper from responsible sources
FSC® C105338

If you have any concerns about our products,
you can contact us on
ProductSafety@springernature.com

In case Publisher is established outside the EU,
the EU authorized representative is:
Springer Nature Customer Service Center GmbH
Europaplatz 3, 69115 Heidelberg, Germany

Printed by Libri Plureos GmbH
in Hamburg, Germany